MORE THAN MEETS THE EYE

VISION IN VERSE

JOSEPH STEPHEN

More Than Meets the Eye
Joseph Stephen
Copyright © 2009-2015 Joseph Stephen. All rights reserved.

Faithful Generations
South Australia, Australia

ISBN: 978-0-9924875-0-8

No part of this book may be reproduced without written permission from the publisher or copyright holder, except in the case of brief quotations embodied in critical articles and reviews. No part of this book may be transmitted in any form or by any means—electronic, mechanical, photocopy, recording, or other—without prior written permission from the publisher or copyright holder.

All Scriptures are taken from The *King James Version* of the Holy Bible.

This book is dedicated to my Golden Girl, Mary Florence. My precious bride is truly a blessing from the Lord. I am grateful God gave me such a suitable helper whose zeal for His truth and desire to live in His will is nothing short of excellent. She is indeed a virtuous woman whose price is far above rubies (Prov. 31:10). Strength and honour are her clothing; and she shall rejoice in time to come (Prov. 31:25). Many daughters have done virtuously, but thou excellest them all (Prov. 31:29). Thank you, dear wife, for your loyalty, love, and patience through the years.

Contents

Foreword ix

Acknowledgments xi

Children and Family. 1
    To My Golden Girl 3
    The Father. 5
    The Heroine Unsung. 8
    A Tribute to Mum 11
    Marriage 13
    Conflict. 16
    A Call to Parents 17
    Unwanted Treasure 20
    Euthanasia. 23
    Children 24
    Evil Eyes (The Scourge of Child Trafficking) 26
    Five Jewels 29
    What I Wish I Was Taught 30
    Thoughts for Young Men. 32
    Thoughts for Young Women 33
    Oh, My Children. 35
    The Mirror. 37
    Family Life. 39
    Home Schooling 43
    The Aussie Community. 45
    Aussie Neighbour. 47
    Christianity and Politics. 49
    The Atom Bomb 51

Struggles ... 55
   Loneliness ... 57
   Singing A Song ... 59
   Blindness ... 61
   This Tree ... 64
   The Victim ... 66
   Titanic - A Poem for Paul ... 70
   Faithful Are the Wounds of a Friend ... 72
   The Warrior ... 73
   Relentless ... 75

Orthodoxy & Orthopraxy ... 77
   Absolute Truth ... 79
   Only One Way ... 82
   The True Gospel ... 83
   Response to the Gospel ... 85
   Faith ... 87
   The Street Preacher ... 89
   Always Somewhere Else ... 91
   Erosion ... 93
   Creation vs. Evolution ... 95
   Environmentalism ... 98
   Be a Man of Your Word ... 101
   Christianity by Name ... 103
   Textbook Christians ... 106
   Orthopraxy ... 108
   Christian Cliques ... 109
   Critical? ... 111
   I Am Nothing (without Love) ... 114
   Christian Liberty ... 116
   Gluttony ... 118
   Culture Transformers ... 120
   Modesty ... 123
   Life's Extremes ... 125
   Taste and See ... 127
   Perseverance ... 128

Fulfilment	131
Every Good and Perfect Gift	132
Ever Mindful	134
Thank You, Lord	136

Epilogue to the 2009 Edition 138

Epilogue to the 2015 Edition 139

Endnotes 143

Foreword

God has created us with many emotions. In no wise is the Christian's life supposed to be void of emotion. Often Christians think that just because they are under the Lordship of Christ they will have no more experience of sadness, frustration, difficulty, or hurt. We are not guaranteed of this and in fact are told to expect tribulation (John 16:33, Eccl. 3:1-11). What we are promised is the Lord's presence through whatever trial He sees fit to allow us to experience in order to mould us into His likeness (Heb. 13:5).

The Christian should be honest, even as David was when he expressed in his psalms such a wide range of feelings as he faced the challenges of life. We should not walk around with a fake smile as so many would have us believe. The Lord Jesus was described as a man of sorrows and acquainted with grief (Isa. 53:3). Joy is not frivolity, but simply inner tranquillity and security in the midst of any raging storm. The victorious Christian life is not a life void of falls or difficulties nor is it one in which we dishonestly hide behind a mask. It is a life in which our faith is not shaken nor our love for God diminished, no matter the trial. It is having the courage to be honest in difficulty, showing dependence on God and others rather than independence. It is having the humility to confess our sin to God and our faults to one another (1 John 1:9, James 5:16). It is having the resolve to continually renew our minds in order to know God's perfect will for us (Rom. 12:2).

As a totally blind father of nine children so far (one already with the Lord), married for seventeen years to a very long-suffering wife, running a home business, and helping my wife home educate our children with a vision for instilling multi-generational faithfulness, these poems have been born out of a rich wealth of experience, both challenging and encouraging. Poetry is a very personal and honest means of communicating our deepest feelings of love, appreciation, joy, grief, or frustration. I share my poetry in the hope that it will help unlock the deepest recesses of your own heart and that you may be able to put into words your own unspoken groanings. I share my poetry as a means of observation, education, challenge, and warning. Many of my poems are purposefully written as mini sermons. At whatever level you analyse my expression, may it be of help to you in some way and to the glory of Almighty God, who enabled us to express our hearts in such a manner.

Acknowledgments

Thank you for choosing this book out of the millions available. I hope you are truly blessed, challenged and encouraged.

I thank my precious bride, Mary Florence, for her hours of proofreading, commenting, and constructive criticism
—Pr. 27:6

I thank my children, a continual fount of laughter and tears and everything in between.

I thank my mother, Karyn Ash, from whom it appears I inherited a love of writing.

I thank Caleb, Gideon and Micah, my three oldest sons, for proofreading this edition of the book.

I thank Dr. Lance Box, Dr. Jean Engela, Theo Engela and David D'Lima for their invaluable suggestions incorporated into this edition.

I thank my Lord and Saviour Jesus Christ, who made my life the poem it is[1].

Children and Family

Lo, children are an heritage of the LORD: and the fruit of the womb is his reward. As arrows are in the hand of a mighty man; so are children of thy youth. Happy is the man that hath his quiver full of them: they shall not be ashamed, but they shall speak with the enemies in the gate.
—Ps. 127:3-5

Blessed is every one that feareth the LORD; that walketh in his ways. For thou shalt eat the labour of thine hands: happy shalt thou be, and it shall be well with thee. Thy wife shall be as a fruitful vine by the sides of thine house: thy children like olive plants round about thy table. Behold, that thus shall the man be blessed that feareth the LORD.
—Ps. 128:1-4

Children's children are the crown of old men; and the glory of children are their fathers.
—Pr. 17:6

He maketh the barren woman to keep house, and to be a joyful mother of children. Praise ye the LORD.
—Ps. 113:9

And he took a child, and set him in the midst of them: and when he had taken him in his arms, he said unto them, Whosoever shall receive one of such children in my name, receiveth me: and whosoever shall receive me, receiveth not me, but him that sent me.
—Mark 9:36-37

To My Golden Girl

Beauty is much more than meets the eye. My dear wife has shown me such patience and loyalty through our marriage in spite of my having a difficult disability to deal with and being a difficult person to live with.

No, not the hair,
No, not the skin,
It's the heart that's solid gold,
That hidden treasure within.
Yes, the outer beauty shines
But it's not just skin deep.
It's beauty through and through,
From the head down to the feet.
Thanks for being you.
For your love, your strength, your self.
God found my perfect friend,
Companion, and faithful help.
Your diligence to seek truth
Your humility to obey,
When all those around you
Just go their merry way.
These aren't just my words,
For the Bible is plainly clear
That reward waits for such as you
Who hold no treasure here.[2]
Love and admiration
Just two words which come to mind

More than Meets the Eye

For my bride and faithful friend
Truly one of a kind.
The mother of my children,
The wife of my youth,
I love you dearly, Florence,
Know this of a truth.

THE FATHER

Every father must be a leader.[3]
We must have deliberate direction.
Our role goes beyond earning the money;[4]
And more than just physical protection.[5]
We must keep the purpose and goals of our family
Firmly fixed in our minds.
Our role of discipleship, nurture, and shepherding,[6]
Must not be left to spare time.
This must be our focus, our subject of prayer,
Our passion, completely consuming.
Our children are far more than just mouths to feed,
Godly seed we must be consciously grooming.[7]

Our other role of husband as well,
Must not be only in name.
The husbandman's job is to care for his garden,
With fruitfulness being his aim.
The Bible says that his wife shall be
Just like a fruitful vine.[8]
His children around the table described
As olive plants and arrows refined.[9]
Our sons as plants grown up in their youth,
Our daughters as palace stones polished,[10]
We must reject any vain "ism" of man
Which sees this distinction demolished.

The husband must always be tender and kind,
And cherish his helpmeet so dear.[11]
God created her equal, but different
To work in a complementary sphere.
Too often today he forces his bride
To be just like another man.
He pushes her hard to work outside,
This is the feminist plan.
But woman's work inside the home[12]
Has higher value than gold,
"She that rocks the cradle," it's said,
"Is the one who changes the world."[13]

So father and husband, consider our role,
Expect it fulfilled by no other.
And encourage your wife that she may be found,
A joyful and virtuous mother.[14]
Work together in this dominion plan,
To raise the next generation.
To fear the Lord and obey His command,[15]
And rebuild a godly nation.

But now back to us fathers,
It's been too long unsaid,
We must take the lead,
We must look ahead.
Nurture is far more than clothing and roof,
It's complete education,
It's preparation for life.[16]
Teach them the scriptures with careful instruction,
Diligently passing on every conviction.
We must learn to be humble,
We must learn to be gentle,[17]
Remembering things are best learned by example.[18]

The Father

Pray for your children.
For their future spouses.
Plead for their hearts,[19]
Against the dark forces.
Pray for great wisdom.[20]
Look well to your going.[21]
For every decision,
Has an outflowing.[22]
Enjoy every year
As you watch them flourish
But don't lose your vision
And see them perish.[23]

THE HEROINE UNSUNG

I confess that this poem is a poor attempt at what is indeed a difficult task, to capture the achievements and unseen labour and love of a mother. To my wife, my childrens' mother, and to every mother, this poem is dedicated to you. I wrote this in response to the headline news of a sixteen- year-old Australian girl circumnavigating the globe solo.

She hasn't sailed solo around the globe,
But she's been up many a night rocking infants alone.[24]
She hasn't had her face splashed across the big screen,
Her many achievements are by the masses unseen.
Her singing isn't heard on the radio,
Yet her voice is the first thing her children will know.
Every child who knows the love of a mum,
Should express adoration to the heroine unsung.

She isn't commanding attention from the big stage,
Her long overtime doesn't triple her wage.
In fact the value placed upon her home role,
Is not recognized by society as a whole.
Her work never ends, she doesn't knock off,
She's always on call, through the calm and the rough.
Take a moment and consider what you've become,
It's time to say thank you to the heroine unsung.

The Heroine Unsung

You won't find her on the cover of a glossy magazine.
She's not strutting her stuff as a beauty queen.
Yet as hidden treasure deep in the earth,
Those who are discerning understand her immense worth!
She's not in the frontline, fighting our wars,
She's busy keeping house behind closed doors.
A man one time wisely observed
That the one who rocks the cradle is the one who rules the world.[25]

Remember the nights when she soothed your fears?
Cleaned up your messes and wiped your tears?
Those sleepless nights of endless feeds,
Cooking, cleaning, providing your needs.
Correcting your tantrums, your bad attitude,
Praising your behaviour when you were good.
You can never remember all she has done,
But you can say thank you to the heroine unsung.

There's one more rare who deserves special note,
For mother of the year I cast in my vote,
She receives every baby that God sends along,
And chooses to educate her children at home,
Her life is poured out for her family and Lord,
For her sacrifice, she'll receive great reward.
She prays that her children, godly become,
She's content to be a heroine unsung.

Through the many years of toil and pain,
The love of a mother will always remain.
Though many things change, friends come and go,
The love of a mother is the deepest you'll know.

More than Meets the Eye

Show her the honour her works so deserve,
Return her the favour of the deepest of love,
For the years of her caring you can't fathom the sum,
Just remember to say thank you to the heroine unsung.

The storms and the billows she has persevered,
None sailing the ocean has even come near.
Marriage and children are for the long haul,
And it takes a special mum to persevere through it all.
Yet it's those who for a season grab the limelight,
And not those who labour by day and by night.
So next time you're tempted to lavish praise on someone,
Remember your mother, the heroine unsung.

A Tribute to Mum

At only seventeen, your life already rough,
You fled a lonely girls' home, looking for some love.
Then you married early, and by the age of twenty-one,
You had birthed a daughter, and a blind and sickly son.

If that was insufficient, your man then let you down,
And along came another, who just seemed to hang around.
Neither really cared about the woman you truly were.
Both only thought of self and the desires you'd stir.

To your blind and sickly son, you gave all that you had.
He only had you, he never knew his dad.
Your daughter too craved the attention from her mother,
Because she saw so little of her problematic father.

Baby number three was born amidst enduring strife,
As man one left the scene, and man two took you as his wife.
Then came another son, and by the age of twenty-eight,
You had four dependent children, but still your heart ached.

Out on the town, ever yearning for a friend,
You met another man, who'd leave you in the end.
From one man to another, you sought a kindred heart,
But all thought of only "self", and ultimately they'd part.

Not every choice you ever made was wise that may be true,
But this is by no means unique to only you.
And not everything that men did, was totally to blame,
Some sober introspection is instructive just the same.

More than Meets the Eye

As time went by, the children left, to go their separate ways,
The men too gone, now left alone, your life was just a haze.
Still seeking your identity, but turning now from men,
You met others burnt like you, looking for a friend.

Once men's lusts were out the way, you finally found the gem,
A friend who cared for who you were, and not what you could
    give them.
And now your sons are older, they too can see right through,
The pain caused by selfish men, to the person that is you.

Though daughter may not be present, her life reflecting yours,
Murdered by a lustful man, her downfall the same cause,
I vow to make a difference, in the way I treat my wife,
To be a friend and love her, to learn from your sad life.

Life is more than "body", we have a heart and soul;
All three need the nurture, and that should be our goal.
But true love is only possible, when God shows us what it is;
In one word, it's "selflessness", the example being His.

So mother dear, realize now, your value is more than gold;
A diamond formed beneath the weight, too precious to be sold.
Your life was not in vain for me, I've learned a thing or two,
And for this wisdom that I've gleaned, I'll always truly love you.

Happy mother's day every day for the rest of your life.

Marriage

A house divided against itself,
Will certainly come to ruin.[26]
God hath made the man and wife,
A single blessed union.[27]
Let not man tear what God hath joined,
No, let there not be schism.[28]
Infighting and disunity,
Will only yield confusion.

The husband cries, "Wife, submit!"[29]
The wife asks, "Where's the love?"[30]
The fingers point, the blame is cast,
A solution seems far off.
Each one of us must guard our hearts[31]
Against pride and selfishness;
For these things often rob the home
Of God's most perfect rest.

Know that when one member hurts,
The whole body feels the pain;
And when one member celebrates,
All the members gain.[32]
Marriage is the union,
Of two members tightly joined;
So when one causes anguish,
He will not escape, be warned.

More than Meets the Eye

Remember, oh, dear husband,
How your master loves the church.
He gave His very life for her
And bestows the highest worth.[33]
The church is never perfect and
His love does not depend
On her actions good or lacking,
He is faithful to the end.

Dwell with your wife in knowledge.
You are joint heirs together.
Your prayers will be hindered,
If you fail to remember.[34]
Give honour to the weaker
And never become bitter.[35]
Shepherd her and show her,
That you'll cherish her forever.

Oh, wife, you are his help meet;[36]
He is your head and your protection.[37]
Bear with him in patience,
In spite of his imperfection.
Encourage him and love him,
Your impact is profound.
A wise woman builds her house,
But the foolish plucks it down.[38]

May your husband safely trust in you,
Look well to all your ways.
Obey the law of kindness and
Do him goodness all his days.[39]
Favour is deceitful
And beauty is truly vain,
But a woman who fears the Lord,
She surely will be praised.[40]

Marriage

It is better to dwell in the wilderness,
Than with a contentious wife;[41]
And as wood is to a fire,
A contentious man will kindle strife.[42]
So stop that drip, drip, dripping.
Oh, woman, please take heed[43]
And man do not be wrathful,
It worketh not the will of God.[44]

Marriage in all is honourable,[45]
It's God's perfect will.
He gave the woman to the man,
This plan is perfect still.
The purpose is to procreate,
A line of godly seed,[46]
Of women meek and virtuous[47]
And visionary men who lead.[48]

Conflict

When the pressure explodes and the shrapnel flies,
We react in defense to our further demise.
Rather than dealing with a problem's real source,
We try in vain to stave off the force.
It happens so often, we don't seem to learn,
The heat from explosion is certain to burn.
There are signs of the buildup which often forewarn,
So alleviate pressure before the storm.
The extent of the damage, time will reveal,
And the scars from such conflict take longer to heal.
Be sensitive and vigilant to the needs of your wife,
To avoid the pain of acrimonious strife.

A Call to Parents

Calling all parents to return to the home,
When it would seem more fulfilling to yonder roam.
To shepherd our children, to nurture their hearts,[49]
To forsake selfish ambition is where it starts.

Oh, dad, you might think your child's life is trite
When he shows you his grasshopper when you come home at night,
When she tells you she found you a pretty flower,
Don't sigh with impatience for their bedtime hour.

Oh, mum, you may think that the chores are mundane,
The mess, the tantrums, the bodily pain.
After all, society despises your role,
And the more children you have just takes its toll.

So today no one has them, or they stop at just one.
We use birth control and murder to ensure they won't come.
And when they are born, our actions speak clear,
We can't wait till they're school-age or can be put in daycare.

Besides, we're taught that the earth is too full.
And this is instilled when they first get to school.
No wonder they feel unwanted and blame,
And the church thinks no different, we're mostly the same.

More than Meets the Eye

Disintegration of the family is rife today.
With one or both parents often away.
The children are raised by their peers or the state,
And the doctrine of humanism seals their fate.[50]

On this one thing most Christians agree
It's a terribly egregious tragedy –
They send out their children to be devoured by wolves,
As they watch them lose their faith in the schools.[51]

Most parents will say they just followed the rest.
They don't stop to consider just what might be best.
They're unaware of God's commandment to educate,[52]
As they surrender their children to the humanist state.

When will we learn that seedlings can't stand
The power of a storm or a blizzard of sand?
Until their roots have grown strong and deep in God's Word,
Exposure like this is plainly absurd.

God clearly assigned us the roles to embrace,
A man's work to provide, his wife's work in the house.[53]
The father as leader should give clear direction,
His wife as his help meet beneath his protection.[54]

The home must again become the center of learning,
Teaching children wisdom, character, to be discerning,
That getting a job is a means, not the end,
That family relationships are more important than friends.

Why are we alarmed in our twilight years?
When our children forsake us in favor of peers?
When we're left to rot in the old folks' home,
Remember how often we left them alone?

A Call to Parents

Remember how we sent them away?
To "educate" them in the fads of the day?
Into a system which taught them that life is about "me,"
That nothing else matters, as long as "I'm happy."

We need reformation in the family sphere,
We need true repentance and godly fear,
Oh, parents we must all turn our hearts toward home,[55]
Or the next generation will yonder roam.

Unwanted Treasure

I realize that it is not always the mother who wants her baby aborted. I feel deep grief for a mother who is forced against her will to end the life of her baby by the baby's irresponsible father or a parent. Whoever it is, it is to them that the sentiment of this poem is directed. If you have aborted your baby, God's forgiveness can be found if you are repentant.

> Knit together in his mother's womb,
> Fearfully and wonderfully made![56]
> Each cell part of a grand design,
> Bearing the image of God.[57]
> Before any shape is seen by the eye,
> There's purpose to each cell divide;[58]
> After only seven weeks' time,
> A baby is recognized.
>
> His toes and fingers visible,
> He stretches arms and legs.
> His little heart pounds with zeal,
> He turns his tiny head.
> His little ears are fully formed,
> His nose so cute and prominent,
> His tiny eyes are still shut tight,
> Every feature evident.[59]

Unwanted Treasure

His world is safe and cosy warm,
Hidden from the sun.
One day this little tiny boy,
Will laugh and play and run.
He swims about and somersaults,
In playful antics free,
He has no reason to fear or feel
Any anxiety.

But harsh the world, outside there's strife,
His mother cold and cruel;
Wants to end his budding life,
Because her life's too full.
She has career and goals so grand,
No time for inconvenience;
As she waits for Doctor Death,
She's encouraged in her vengeance.

Suddenly he feels sharp pain,
There's no place for him to turn.
Even if he could scream aloud,
His cry the world would spurn.
The doctor's mission near complete,
He writhes to be set free;
Relentless are the tools of death,
Until finally they succeed.

Instead of into arms of love,
He's cast into the dirt.
After all he's a lump of cells,
According to Doctor Expert.

His precious soul is then released,
And to his God returns.
"My dearest child, you're welcome here,
Come join the growing throng.

"My precious child, you are so dear,
There's none with higher worth.
I've told mankind what I think of you,
It's published in all the earth.[60]
"When I came down and dwelt with man,[61]
I held children to my heart.[62]
When they rejected you, my anger burned![63]
You were precious from the start."

From conception life indeed begins,
Before the heart's first beat,
Before appearance of head or limbs,
You are a human life unique.
Every life is sacred,
No matter how young or old.
Hark, the lonely helpless cry,
And defend the unborn child!

Euthanasia

If your grandma is ill and on you she relies,
There's a modern solution: just euthanize.
If the burden of your disabled child you despise,
There's a "compassionate" answer: just euthanize.
Unwanted children we abort without flinching our eyes,
And unwanted adults we'll just euthanize.

"Oh," you might say, "but they want euthanasia."
Of course, when you remind them they're taking your leisure.
When they're made to feel unwanted and better off dead,
When they're told that they're taking up a hospital bed,
When they're vulnerable and weak at their moment of need,
You plant in their mind that diabolical seed.[64]

But what about those who are racked with pain,
Who want for their lives to just come to an end?
There's palliative care and pain relief,
Surrounded by loved ones in the midst of their grief.
Regardless of reason, we don't have the right
To murder a person, whatever his plight.[65]

What happened, oh, man, to the sanctity of life?[66]
Our value is reduced to utilitarian price.
Birth control, abortion, and now one step further—
Any feeble excuse, we can legally murder.
The boundaries move slowly, like the tide of the sea,
Till murder is legal just to make someone happy.

Children

Children are blessings from the Lord
According to His holy Word.
As arrows in the warrior's hands
Sharpened by training in God's commands.[67]

Just as they sacrificed their sons of old,
Career and lifestyle are the gods of gold.[68]
Abortion and the use of birth control
Are the modern fires, which take their toll.

If we love God, our hearts should grieve.
We should love what He loves, if we believe.
God loves children, He hath said,[69]
Yet even Christians want dogs instead.

Some may ask who will provide?
Faith and wisdom will decide.
One who works, who chooses well,
To them the floodgates are opened wide.[70]

Take note of the psalms
As David said,
"The righteous not forsaken,
Nor his seed begging bread."[71]

Children

Today it seems the tables are turned:
The barren are blessed and the fruitful are scorned;[72]
But whatever our worldview, God's Word hasn't changed.
Humanism and feminism are now what is learned.

How far we've strayed from God's holy plan
And forgotten the first task given to man.[73]
Did you know, overpopulation is just a lie,[74]
Our selfish lifestyles to justify.

If we would raise up godly seed
And train up warriors who can lead,
Revival would spread across the land,
The difference made would be profound.

Even Muslims know this rule,[75]
Yet Christians have learned from the wrong school.
It's time to stop believing the lie
And be fruitful and multiply.

Evil Eyes
(The Scourge of Child Trafficking)

Thousands of innocent children each day
Are forced into bondage and traded as slaves.
Snatched from their families and sent far away,
To gratify lusts of the rich and depraved.

Impoverished families peddle their children,
Who are promised an affluent future.
But what happens to each precious treasure,
Is hell upon earth beyond measure.

It's worse than abortion for they go on enduring,
Longing for parents to comfort their fears,
Their abusers unfeeling, their pain unrelenting.
Hardened by cruelty, futile their tears.

Starved and tortured, their innocence stolen,
Savagely assaulted, their spirit broken.
Forced to serve men, daily more than a dozen,[76]
Discarded as refuse, their lives left in ruin.

Complacent, we think that Wilberforce triumphed,
Slavery abolished through his diligent stand,
A million times worse, it goes on unabated,[77]
While Christians relax with their head in the sand.

Lulled into thinking our children invulnerable,
Nothing can touch them, "It won't happen to me."
But even around you, evil eyes may be watching,
Waiting for just the right opportunity.

Evil Eyes (The Scourge of Child Trafficking)

It's somebody's daughter, it's somebody's son,
It's not just a nameless, faceless one.
Not just a statistic, a number out there,
Each one of them precious, each one of them dear.

Most go unreported where nobody cares,
Only the rich get attention for theirs.
A handful are rescued but forever scarred,
But the cry of the majority continues unheard.

The tragedy too is just who is involved.
It explains why such cases are rarely solved.
Judges, policemen, politicians as well[78]
All contribute to this network from hell.

Be vigilant, oh, parent, be on your guard.
No child is safe, even in their backyard.
But knowledge is power in the hands of the wise,
Our children must learn that snares are disguised.

Don't blame God for man's depraved action.
He made all things good at the start of creation.
He gave us laws for our own protection,
But our hearts are deceitful with wicked affection.[79]

We despise God's law, it "stifles expression,"
Unless someone's crime threatens our freedom.
We would rather be free from law's bounding fence,
And then blame God with the sad consequence.

It's time to make a bold stand in the church,
To speak against the pornographical scourge.
But it plagues many pastors just the same,[80]
So the church remains silent to its own shame.

More than Meets the Eye

Empty the closet of skeleton bones.
Take stock of the media that fill our homes.
Remove the fuel and extinguish the flame.
Till this sin is forsaken, we're part of the blame.

As Christians we must do all that we can
To stop this self-centred satisfaction of man.
It starts with us teaching the next generation
To value and protect all women and children.

The promiscuous culture amongst our youth
Must be transformed by the gospel's truth,
Or they might just be the ones willing to pay,
To defile your own precious child one day.

Five Jewels

    This poem was written after the death of our second daughter, Esther Ruth, Hannah's twin.

> God lent us five most precious jewels.
> One loaned for just two days.
> We cuddled her and felt a bond,
> That time cannot erase.
>
> Her short stay taught us life's a gift,
> To treasure those whom God has left—
> Our other jewels, her sister twin,
> Caleb, Micah, Gideon.
>
> Four jewels entrusted to our care
> Whom we hope will meet her there.
> But we must teach with diligence,
> The way of faith and repentance.
>
> Esther Ruth has gone ahead,
> To her mansion glorious.
> We pray the four will trust the Lord,
> And not live life oblivious.
>
> Our mission then is very clear,
> Instill wisdom, reverence, and holy fear
> Through Esther's life though short and sad
> So all five jewels return to God.

What I Wish I Was Taught

I wish I was taught
How to treat women.
I wish I was taught
What God thinks of children.
I wish I was taught
My role as a father
Was much more than just financial provision.

I wish I was taught
How to disciple.
I wish I was taught
How to have vision.
I wish I was taught
To think like a Christian
And not be persuaded by every delusion.

I wish I was taught
How to save money.
I wish I was taught
How to be patient.
I wish I was taught
Practical living
Like growing a garden and fixing an engine.

I wish I was taught
Not to waste time.
I wish I was taught

What I Wish I Was Taught

To have self-control.
I wish I was taught
To manage my tongue
And not to always have the last say.

Thank God for His mercy.
I'm learning these lessons,
But how much better,
To have learned them much sooner.
One thing's for certain,
I'll teach them my children,
That they will succeed in the next generation.

He that will walk
With wise men shall be wise,
But a companion of fools
Shall be destroyed.[81]
Spend time with those parents
Who have already borne good fruit
And learn by example from experience and wisdom.

Young man or young woman,
Pay close attention.
Use all your free time
In preparation.
The role of a parent
Is of utmost importance,
To raise godly children is your primary mission.[82]

Thoughts for Young Men

Transfixed by her beauty, a deception of old,
Take heed to this wisdom, all glitter is not gold.
The lips that drop honeycomb, they're smoother than oil,
But her end bitter wormwood, a two-edge'd sword.[83]
Lust not for her beauty, those fluttering eyes,
Many young men have made choices unwise.[84]
It's too easy then to walk out and change course,
But know this beloved, God hates divorce.[85]

Beneath the façade of beauty and smell,
Is there a virtuous woman or a Jezebel?[86]
What is important isn't drawn on her face,
Does she honour her parents? Treat siblings with grace?
Is her love for God shown in bearing her cross?
Is she willing to count earthly treasure as loss?
Is she willing to follow you where God may lead?
Is her primary focus to raise godly seed?[87]

Of course you too must be the right man,
Your primary purpose to fulfill God's plan;[88]
To cherish and nurture her in sickness and health,
To pursue godliness, not status and wealth;[89]
Not to wander when her luster is spent,
But as time passes, to continue content.[90]
Of pastures greener others may boast,
But the grass will be greenest where you water it most.

Thoughts for Young Women

Tall, dark and handsome, his charisma contagious,
He'll tug at your heart strings with emotion voracious.
He'll woo you with flowers or a ring with a stone,
And make every effort to get you alone.

He'll make you think you're the first he has dated,
But soon you'll realise that value deflated.
Once he has used you he'll discard you like dirt.
And look for another with whom he can flirt.

You weren't the first girl to fan his flame,
And a street-wise flirt may play his game;
But a godly girl should stay far from his net,
Or your unwise choices you will live to regret.

Your conduct also must send the right signal,
With modest deportment and a spirit that's gentle;[91]
Not seeking attention from the wrong kind of people,
Displaying wisdom as a godly example.

It is said that the difference between men and boys
Is the time and money spent on their toys;
But where his treasure is, there is his heart,[92]
So take careful note of this right from the start.

Something to look for when examining traits,
Is who sets his direction, God or his mates?[93]
And is he hard-working or slothful and slack?
Don't think you will change him some time down the track.

When the right kind of man approaches your father,[94]
A man who shows humble respect to his mother,
With practical skills and a knowledge of Scripture,[95]
It is this kind of husband who'll make a good leader.

Though in your journey you both seek God's will,
Satan will tempt you and buffet you still.
Keep Christ at the center to remain unshaken,
For a threefold cord is not easily broken.[96]

Oh, My Children

At the time I wrote this poem we had seven children, including Esther, who was already with the Lord.

Oh, my children, look to me.
Let your eyes observe my ways.[97]
Let me show you wondrous things,
That your mouth be full of praise:

Not for me or what I do,
But for your God so awesome,
That you'll catch the vision of His truth,
And pass it to your children.[98]

Do not forget how He hath led,
Your parents in their journey.
Nor how He provided for every need
And always showed us mercy.

No, don't forget His sacrifice,
His compassion, nor His love
How He gave His very life for us,
And prepareth mansions up above.[99]

We have done nothing to deserve
His mercy or His grace,
Yet faith in Him alone will save:[100]
My children, look into His face.[101]

More than Meets the Eye

When sin besets, and it will,
When temptation tugs the heart,
When the easy life seems inviting,
When you're feeling torn apart,

Remember this life is very short.
It's nothing to compare
With the eons of eternity.
So soon we'll all be there.

The trials of this present life
By comparison are very small
To the weight of glory promised then[102]
For His children, one and all.

Yes, look to me my cherished ones,
Though no picture of perfection,
I'll guide and train you by His grace
With much love and affection.

The Mirror

Children are the best mirrors. They reflect with brutal honesty what we really are teaching them and it's not always what we preach. This is often the root cause of why parents fail in their training.

They copy our looks, our tone of voice,
Our impatience and more than warranted force.
They reflect our terrible attitude,
And speak with the same ingratitude.
They do what we do, and not what we say,
Have we taken stock in the mirror today?

When we praise God in one breath and curse in the next,
When we shout at our wife and are easily vexed,
When we keep silent instead of sharing the truth,
When we are unfriendly and behave aloof:
No matter what we preach, what comes out of our mouth,
The faithful mirror reflects our life.

If we want to teach humility,
Godliness, patience, integrity,
If we want to raise godly seed,
It starts with us and how we lead.
What we are is what they'll be,
The mirror is there for all to see.

More than Meets the Eye

Train up a child in the way he should go,
And when he is old he will not depart.[103]
Be not deceived, we'll reap what we sow,[104]
Let's live by example the life to impart.
If we want our training to yield success,
Keep an eye in the mirror for the true progress.

Family Life

This poem was written after reviewing my journal of funny things the children said or did when they were toddlers. Every statement is completely true.

Caleb Sylverius,
Our firstborn son,
Liked to play music
And bang on a drum.
One day as he sat,
Playing in front of us,
He exclaimed, "Mummy,
I'm a concussionist!"

Gideon, two, asked if millipedes bite,
We told him no, but they certainly smell.
As he sat on the pot, after dinner one night,
The silence was broken by a desperate yell.
As he sat on that pot, emptying his tummy,
He shouted, "There's a millipede coming
And it'll smell me, Mummy."

Micah, our third son,
Is quiet and tenacious,
His will is steely strong.
He'll try at length till he's solved his puzzle,
It doesn't matter how long.
One day as he sat sorting the pieces,
With his usual deliberate knowhow,
Mummy asked him what he was doing,
He explained he was fixing the cow.

More than Meets the Eye

Hannah Irene, our firstborn girl,
Has brought to her parents, many a smile.
One night when she was just twelve months young,
While sleeping with us as was her usual style,[105]
She awoke and sat up, next to her mother,
And matter of factly announced, "Bother."
Then lay back down and fell fast asleep,
And for the rest of the night we heard not a peep.

Hannah's twin, Esther Ruth, now at home with our Lord,
Was with us for only two days.
We held her and felt the pain of her parting,
For her short life we still give God praise.
Such contradiction of death, so soon after birth,
But duration of life does not diminish her worth.
Esther we see in the eyes of her sister.
No matter the time we'll always miss her.

Amos, oh, Amos, that toddler boy,
Has brought much laughter, tears, and joy.
When asked where his airplane slippers were one day,
He looked up and said, "They flew away."
He roars and crawls around like a lion.
He goes spelunking under the bed.
He stands on my shoulders pretending he's flying.
He's always hungry as if never fed.

Smiley faced Moses, his affection so warm,
Brightens the morning with his cheerful song.
When I'm cumbered with work, ready to snap,
Along comes Moses and climbs on my lap.
It's "Roses for Moses", "Geraniums for Dad",
When Moses is happy, who can be sad?
Tongue-tied from birth, he was slow off the mark,
But what joy now radiates from this little spark.

Family Life

Disappointed that Moses might be our last,
Noah, born at home, arrived with a blast.
A toy in his mouth, a book in each hand,
He'd crawl to daddy, and then try and stand.
When exhausted I finally get to bed for some rest,
He wakes up and won't sleep unless he's on daddy's chest.
The baby of the family, his antics enthrall,
The delight of his siblings, he's adored by us all.

But wait, as they say, there's more to tell,
Three years later came another baby girl!
Abigail Faith with her cute little squeal,
Sucks her knuckles as we eat our meal.
She'll gaze intensely to catch your eye,
And if you don't respond she'll begin to cry.
Show her a flower and her mouth opens wide,
As she tastes it then buries her nose inside.

Soldiers and cowboys or tea parties grand,
Lego, Meccano, woodwork, or sand,
Cars and trucks or horses and dolls,
Skinned knees, banged heads, or grazes and falls,
Cooking, cleaning, sweeping the floors,
Washing, folding, tidying the drawers.
Working, playing, peace or strife,
This is children. This is family life.

Studying the Scriptures around the table,
Praying at bed-time, the young ones are able.
Giving thanks to God for His daily provision,
They sleep secure, knowing parents' affection.
Mummy and Daddy are exhausted but glad,
That God has so blessed us with the children we've had.
Family life is a challenge indeed,
With its critical mission to raise godly seed.

More than Meets the Eye

It's not always laughs, it's not always play.
There are tears when they're stubborn and disobey.
It's often hard work, there are sleepless nights.
There's sometimes arguing and sometimes fights.
There's lots of training and lots of correcting.
Our own imperfections we see them reflecting.
But children are blessings, there is no doubt.
And not one we'd imagine being without.

Home Schooling

Folding the washing,
Preparing the food,
Reciting times tables,
Discussing God's Word,
Caring for baby,
Sweeping the floor,
Whatever we're learning,
This is home schooling.

Working together,
Older and younger,
Building character,
Discipling as mentor.
Line upon line,[106]
Gradually growing,
Relationships strengthened,
This is home schooling.

Education is more
Than just learning facts.
It's submitting to authority
And learning respect.
It's teaching life skills,
To be persevering.
It's leading by example.
This is home schooling.

More than Meets the Eye

Patiently practising
Piano, violin.
Diligently drawing
Or colouring in.
Science experiments,
Very intriguing,
Comprehension or spelling,
This is home schooling.

Weeding or planting,
Hoeing or digging,
Painting or sanding,
Nailing or drilling,
Sewing a button,
Practical learning,
Whatever is useful,
This is home schooling.

Reading or writing,
Work is exciting.
There's purpose to learning,
For future preparing.
From the moment of waking,
Till just before sleeping,
Whatever we're doing,
This is home schooling.

The Aussie Community

The definition of the Aussie community
Is to live as far from one's neighbour as possible.
To not see, hear, or know what is happening
To the people who share the local proximity.

In new suburbs the blocks are incredibly small,
Yet between every house is constructed a wall.
The only time there's contact over the fence
Is if your neighbour with you has a grievance.

On the roads it's road rage.
In the shops no courtesy.
At the door it's indifference.
In the media it's fantasy.

Even the church has redefined fellowship,
And hospitality is becoming a lost art.
When we get together for a communal meal
We bring our own and sit apart.

In another culture the saying goes,
"It takes a village to raise a child."
In Australia though, nobody knows
Or cares if a youngster grows up wild.

More than Meets the Eye

Who defined community as individuality?
Why has greeting become insincerity?
Where is the support of extended family?
What will we leave but a tragic legacy?

When people do talk, it's about the weather,
And the superficiality goes no further.
We're so afraid to open our hearts,
But this is where community starts.

AUSSIE NEIGHBOUR

Dear Aussie neighbour, may I humbly appeal
Who issued the command that "Thou shalt not steal?"[107]
When one is robbed of a hard earned possession,
Who isn't incensed and filled with frustration?

And then, Aussie neighbour, how would you feel
If one of your family was brutally killed?[108]
If one took the life of your son or your daughter?
Who uttered the words that "Thou shalt not murder?"[109]

Oh, Aussie neighbour, have you thought about this?
Who declared it is wrong to bear false witness?[110]
Does time negate testimony or make truth a lie?
Is the guilty made innocent with the wink of an eye?

The foundation of our law is from Almighty God
Not Muhammad nor Buddha, nor who's in the top job.[111]
We're reaping the decay of the slippery slide
Of denying this truth in arrogant pride.

We take it for granted, the word of a mate,
Trust is crucial for prosperity to thrive.
Where truth is not the foundation of the State,
Corruption is the only way to survive.[112]

More than Meets the Eye

We want Christian values but deny their source,
We love the law when it protects our right.
We cry "injustice!" when the law's not enforced,
But when we're the guilty, for change we will fight.

We're casting away, with no second thought,
The source of those values which made us so great,
We embrace all religions, "all equal," we're taught,
Soon Sharia Law will too be our fate.

Freedom of religion was not ever meant
For blasphemy against the One heaven sent.
It was for the worship of God unrestrained,
Not to write laws to make the holy profaned.

These commandments we cherish came from The Book
That most think is fable with no second look.
If that be the case, then so too are these laws,
There's no room for complaint, no pleading your cause.

If it feels good for one to sin against you,
If there are no absolutes, you can't argue.
Whether raping or murder, lying or theft,
You have no recourse, there is no appeal left.

Dear Aussie neighbour, may I finally conclude
Learn from our forefathers, God's ways are for our good.
Our constitution's preamble must be our lifeblood,
"Humbly relying on the blessing of God."[113]

Christianity and Politics

Written after the 21 August, 2010 Australian federal election at which Joseph ran as a senate candidate for South Australia for The Christian Democratic Party, the only unashamedly Christian party in Australia. This is dedicated to the Hon. Fred Nile, founder of CDP, for his faithful service over the past nearly thirty years, a voice crying in the wilderness, one voice standing for truth against the ever growing din of atheism.

God in His sovereignty has allowed a democracy
To enforce His own law, not man's which are arbitrary.[114]
But when Christians shrink back from this grave responsibility,
The wicked will rule because of our apathy.[115]

There's no point praying for our leaders when
There's no one willing to be one of them.
When we're more concerned about our prosperity
Than to stand in the gap and protect God's verity.

Our Christian freedoms are vanishing away,
While we sit in our meetings and continue to pray.
And when they're gone, there'll be no one to blame
But the very Christians who call on God's name.

Our nation, once Christian, the preamble said,
"humbly relying on Almighty God."[116]
But peace and affluence have taken their toll,
and pride and idolatry have caused us to fall.

We still have religion but not the true sort,
Today it's our lifestyle and the god of sport.
The church of God has fallen asleep,
Lulled by carnality and complacency deep.

Wake up, oh, soldiers, oh, army of God,
The Muslims aren't sleeping, nor the atheist mob.
They're marching with vengeance, their swords ready drawn,
They're taking our freedoms, some already gone.

It wasn't Islam which gave us our great prosperity.
Nor the Dalai Lama our vast charity.[117]
We have the God of the Bible to thank for this nation.
Let's not forget our Christian foundation.

You may argue that you weren't called to lead.
Then stand behind those who are willing to bleed.
The Lord Jesus made it abundantly clear,
He'll deny you in heaven if you deny Him down here.[118]

You give them the mandate each time you vote.
And when you decline, the wicked will not.
You will be accountable because of your choice.[119]
As Christians we must cry out with a united voice.

So pray for our leaders, yes, pray indeed.[120]
But vote for a Christian or be willing to lead.
And teach your children their Christian heritage,[121]
So they do not despise their great privilege.

THE ATOM BOMB

The stark reality
Of the change in society
Cuts to the bone
When you look out your window
And there are no children playing,
No laughter or chatter,
No shouts or singing,
Where have the children gone?

A mother plays at home with her children
In a street of misfits.
Two women live one side.
A divorcee the other.
A childless couple behind.[122]
There are no mothers to visit
And no playmates for her children.
The isolation is unkind.

On many a corner
There's a childcare center
With children running riot,
Like *Lord of the Flies*.[123]
When they first come, they're sweet.
When they leave, they're streetwise.

These are our future
What hope do they have?
No loving guidance
No one-to-one care
Imprisoned in this building
Out of mum and dad's hair.

But what choice do we have?
Cost of living is high
Two workers for one.[124]
This is progress
What a lie.

Who teaches the children
In these early years?
It's left to the state
And influence of peers.
Parents are busy,
They just don't have time.
Divorce rate is rising
And so is street crime.

What can we do
when truth is discarded?
God's Word holds the answers
But from this we've departed.
Even the church has lost sight of His way,
And until it returns, we'll see atomic decay.

The Atom Bomb

Older women teaching younger
To be keepers at home,
To love their husbands and children,[125]
And to value this role.
But men have played tyrant and women revolted.
Now society is crumbling and truth is assaulted.

Restore the family for our future's sake.
What kind of leaders will our children make
If they're left to the mercy
Of chaos and crime?
We'll reap what we sow.
It will show in time.

A father providing.
Mother keeping the home.
Obedient children.
And the love of God known.
The atom of society
Is the family alone
But when it is split,
It's an atom bomb.[126]

Struggles

But we glory in tribulations also: knowing that tribulation worketh patience; And patience, experience; and experience, hope: And hope maketh not ashamed; because the love of God is shed abroad in our hearts by the Holy Ghost which is given unto us.

—Rom. 5:3b-5

Blessed be God, even the Father of our Lord Jesus Christ, the Father of mercies, and the God of all comfort; Who comforteth us in all our tribulation, that we may be able to comfort them which are in any trouble, by the comfort wherewith we ourselves are comforted of God.

—2 Cor. 1:3-4

Loneliness

Our family stands out. My wife is originally from Malaysia and I am totally blind. We also have lots of children (five living at the time of this writing) which is unusual for our generation. This poem expresses the loneliness expressed particularly by my wife in her earlier years, but also at times for myself. It is only through experience that we are truly able to comfort others as without the experience, our compassion is often very shallow.

People always talking,
But not to me,
Like looking for fresh water,
In the middle of the sea.

Alone in the crowds,
Alone in my family,
Alone in the church,
And in a strange country.

People always looking.
We're a curiosity,
An exhibit of strange interest
That people pay to see.

Misunderstood, misrepresented,
Different from the rest.
Culturally not accepted
And so obviously expressed.

More than Meets the Eye

Lord Jesus, a man of sorrows,[127]
Was rejected and despised,
Knows loneliness at its worst,[128]
And can truly empathize.[129]

My Lord, let not me fail to be
There for others who are just like me.
Let thy consolation flow
To another heart that's feeling low.

Singing A Song

I certainly don't choose to feel this way,
When I wake up and feel depressed each day.
I consider the throngs of faithless men,
Recklessly rushing to a Christless end.
The church is complacent, singing a song,
And seems unaware that there's anything wrong.

Millions of babies are aborted each year,
With barely a protest or shedding a tear.
Then there are thousands of children abused,
Trafficked for lust then discarded when used.
The church just continues singing her song,
As if unaware that there's anything wrong.

But even within, the problems abound,
Changes are subtle yet highly profound.
The door was left open, key in the lock,
Wolves have crept in to devour the flock.
We go on merrily singing our song,
Oblivious that there's anything wrong.

Those who are different we coldly ignore,
In the too hard basket to build rapport.
The only people to whom we relate:
Are of the same colour and social state.
The church is happily singing her song,
Still unaware that there's anything wrong.

More than Meets the Eye

A troubled man tragically takes his life,
His existence lonely and filled with strife.[130]
No one notices he's missing one day,
Conversation goes on the usual way.
The church is indifferent, singing her song,
Why can't we see that there's anything wrong?

Blindness

I never knew the impact my disability would have on another person until I got married and had children. Over the years we have learned to deal with this unanticipated difficulty, but it's still not easy. I wrote this poem as a means of education rather than complaint or discontentment. I have learned to be content with my lot and recognize that God has allowed me to be this way for His glory and seek to glorify Him in every aspect of my life.

> And the LORD said unto him, Who hath made man's mouth? or who maketh the dumb, or deaf, or the seeing, or the blind? have not I the LORD?
> —Ex. 4:11

It's not that I want sympathy,
But I do want understanding.
Being blind has many difficulties,
Especially for a family.

I can't zip up to the shop,
When we unexpectedly run out of milk.
I can't kick a ball with the children,
Or take them to the park.[131]

I can't bandage a bleeding finger
Or see the extent of a wound.
I can't watch food cooking on the stove,[132]
Or catch a baby falling to the ground.

More than Meets the Eye

I can't drop my wife off
When the carpark is too full
And drive the children around
Till she's finished buying food.

She can't drop me off
At an unfamiliar stall,
Or ask me to find a table
In a crowded food mall.

Yes, there are lots of things I can do
But I can't do so much more.
They don't balance each other out.
Don't reason with me that way.

My dear wife and children
Must compensate my eyes.
My child leads me round the hardware store,
My wife has no choice but to drive.

Your offers of help are appreciated.
Please follow through with your pledge.
It's better if you see what needs doing
To relieve the tension and edge.

Don't get me wrong, I'm not complaining.
There are many worse off than us.
I'm writing this as education
Because things aren't always obvious.

I'm writing so you know how my wife feels,
So you know how tired she gets.
Everything depends on her eyes,
It often fills life with stress.

BLINDNESS

I can change a baby's nappy.[133]
I can bathe and dress the children.
Yes, I can make wooden toys,
Play hide-and-seek and hug them.

This is not about what I can do.
For these things I don't need help.
It's to educate and explain what is hard,
Which makes life so difficult.

When you're blind things take longer:
Going shopping, finding a toilet,
Reading the mail, paying the bills,
Cleaning up the house and garden,
Cooking the meals.

I don't need more advice,
I'm not asking for a solution.
I'm explaining things so you can understand;
To reduce people's expectation.

Being blind is hard, there's no doubt,
Especially with a family.
Please try and remember our plight.
We need your understanding.

This Tree

For the good that I would I do not: but the evil which I would not, that I do. Now if I do that I would not, it is no more I that do it, but sin that dwelleth in me. I find then a law, that, when I would do good, evil is present with me. For I delight in the law of God after the inward man: But I see another law in my members, warring against the law of my mind, and bringing me into captivity to the law of sin which is in my members. O wretched man that I am! who shall deliver me from the body of this death? I thank God through Jesus Christ our Lord. So then with the mind I myself serve the law of God; but with the flesh the law of sin. There is therefore now no condemnation to them which are in Christ Jesus, who walk not after the flesh, but after the Spirit.
—Rom. 7:19-8:1

For a just man falleth seven times, and riseth up again . . . .
—Prov. 24:16

Now no chastening for the present seemeth to be joyous, but grievous: nevertheless afterward it yieldeth the peaceable fruit of righteousness unto them which are exercised thereby.
—Heb. 12:11

My Gardener's tools are sharp and precise—
His pruning is ornate.
His careful hand and His watchful eye
Mould my character and state.

This Tree

Slowly, slowly the dead leaves fall,
Pruned away with care.
The pain, the pain as He works with love.
The dead leaves disappear.

Self, pride, rage, and blame
Must be cut away;
The agony of lessons learnt
And the time it takes to grow.

This tree's fruit is sparse and few
In spite of the Gardener's tending,
But over time and by His grace
This tree is still upstanding.

Seasons come and seasons go.
The same bad fruit appears.
Patiently He trims away
The pain, the falling tears.

Yet He prunes, waters, and His Son still shines.
Sometimes I wonder why
He doesn't uproot this tree
And throw it in the fire.

By His grace, I'll live and learn
As long as He keeps correcting.
Over time I pray He sees
The face of His Son reflecting.

The Victim

My sister was brutally murdered.[134]
My precious daughter died.[135]
Born blind with cerebral palsy,[136]
I could be bitter inside.
People have often inquired
How I could believe in a God
Who claims to be all knowing and loving,[137]
When life has been dreadfully sad.

Born into physical violence,
My biological father unknown,
My mother did her utmost to raise us,
To give us love and a home.
Three marriages each one a failure,
She suffers from mental torment.
Oh, how I longed for a family,
That was normal, loving, and decent.

I often feel grievous rejection,
An intense sadness and pain.
My blindness is a constant burden,
To my loved ones who suffer its bane.
My heart breaks aching and lonely,
Yearning for my family's relief.
My prayers are monotonous pleading,
Crying out through gritted teeth.

The Victim

But my life has imparted perspective,
An empathy for others who hurt,[138]
I feel for the down and the broken,
Who rise up and shake off the dirt.[139]
Evil comes from our choices[140]
And is not the desire of God.[141]
But what He allows us to suffer
He turns around for our good.[142]

We cannot change what has happened,
But we can choose the way we react.
The bruises and scars of our trauma,
Are painful; there's no denying that fact.
But though others may choose to do evil,
We need not continue their shame,
We must move onward and upward,
And quit trying to cast the blame.

The Lord Jesus deserved only worship,[143]
Yet received shameful spitting and scorn.[144]
At His birth He should have been honoured,
But in a manger was humbly born.[145]
In spite of all whom He succored,
He was alone in his torturous death.[146]
Showing concern for his mother,
As He drew His final breath.[147]

Yes, I can believe in a Saviour,
Who loved me enough to die.
Who lived a life amongst evil,
Who suffered far worse than I.

More than Meets the Eye

At heart I'm no different from others
Who've carried out heinous crimes,
I've broken His every commandment,[148]
Not once but thousands of times.

It is God who is truly the victim,
For He created everything good.[149]
We showed Him nothing but hatred,[150]
It was we who shed innocent blood.
His law He gave for protection
That all get the best out of life.
We balk at its cramping restriction,
Then blame Him for lawless strife.

It's foolish to deny His existence
Because we've suffered some pain;
To ignore His obvious presence,
When our conscience burns with His flame.
To try and get by without Him
Is folly of the greatest extreme,
Life is so empty without Him,
An inescapable, horrible dream.

I love to smell God's fragrant roses,
To feel His sun on my face,
To cuddle my newborn baby,
Or be drawn in a loving embrace.
His power is all around me,
The evidence of incredible design,[151]
The testimony of men throughout history,
His written Word truly divine.

The Victim

You ask me why I'm not bitter,
Why I don't think God is to blame?
I entered this world with nothing,
And will leave it with exactly the same.[152]
Everything sent is a blessing.
Upon everyone cometh the rain.[153]
My job is to praise my creator,
Amidst happiness, sorrow, or pain.

Titanic - A Poem for Paul

For the 1st anniversary of my sister Rachele's death 29 March, 2014.
To Paul Richard Wheeler, who was convicted on 18 February, 2014 of Rachele's manslaughter.
(Emergency call evidence presented during his trial clearly exhibited premeditated action.[154])
He was sentenced on 8 August, 2014 for 15 years with a minimum non parole period of 12 years, plus a 10 month revoked suspended sentence to be served for other prior offenses.

In drunken rage, her life destroyed,
Remaining now, an aching void.
Her children left without their mother,
A sister taken from a brother,
A mother longing for her daughter,
Families crushed by brutal slaughter.
May you understand in time,
The pain from this titanic crime.

A troubled soul, indeed she was,
But that is insufficient cause.
To snatch away my sister's life,
With a Wiltshire stay-sharp knife.
You rushed her to a tragic end,
Yet claimed to be her loyal friend.
Then in court you dare to plead,
That you're the victim to be believed.

Titanic - A Poem for Paul

So common oh this line of thought,
So many victims left distraught!
Their perpetrators spin a yarn,
To paint them target of the harm.
Defense then give their story clout
And the jury is swayed by seeds of doubt.
So justice fails to bring relief,
For the victim and their family's grief.

I pray good comes from tragedy.
Perhaps you will be brought to see,
That manliness is self-control,
Not drinking lots of alcohol,
Then showing muscle in a fight,
And using women every night.
Please learn from the Titanic's worst,
Men put women and children first.

Faithful Are the Wounds of a Friend

Faithful are the wounds of a friend,
But deceitful are the kisses of an enemy.[155]
Words of truth that cause pain,
Are better than the praises of flattery.
We all are attracted to superficiality,
But smiles and hugs do not equate to honesty.
Dangerous is contempt bred through familiarity,
But people come and go, so don't despise your family.

The mirror never lies, and pride it will deflate,
But truth offers hope, so don't deny its honesty.
We prefer inspiring words than to be put straight,
But better the reproof than the consequence of vanity.
If we respond to correction in humility
And are thankful for the stripes of sincerity,
If we accept that chastening is charity,
Our character will be strengthened—so too our integrity.

Be thankful for the ones who dare to speak truth.
Overlook the times when they seem to be rough.
The chisel of chastening can cut to the heart,
But living a delusion is not very smart.
It's better to know that you need some correction
Than to live a lie in the midst of affection.
So treasure the friend who cares for your soul
And not flattering words and a dishonest smile.

The Warrior

The battle is fierce,
And one fights alone,
Without reinforcement,
Reclaiming lost ground.

Day in and day out,
This warrior must fight,
Keeping a watch
All hours of the night.

Skilfully using the sword and the shield,[156]
Denying the comforts as the will learns to yield.
Weary and frail, but faithfully still,
Enduring the hardship, lonely and ill.

Falling on knees,
Enduring the pain,
The enemy flees,
The fight's not in vain.

For many, this warrior has made sacrifice,
But they're unaware of the battle's high cost.
They know not the endurance of the warrior's toil
But eagerly enjoy the fruit of the spoil.

When freedom's secured, when all is at peace,
It's others who usually are seen as the source.
But when you see victory and bitter wars cease,
Remember the warriors and their formidable force.

Who is this warrior whose virtues I praise,
Whose faithful commitment by most is unknown?
Not in the limelight, hidden for days,
It's the elderly lady who prays in her home.

(This poem is dedicated to the late Edie Richardson, the late Olga Sulyma, Mary Wilkins, the late Irma Naughton, and all other prayer warriors. Thank you for your prayers [1 Thess. 5:17; Eph. 6:18; 1 Peter 3:12; Luke 2:36–38].)

Relentless

With stealth he prowls, no warning growls,
He waits with latent power.
To catch a weary saint off guard,
To savagely devour.[157]
We're rarely ready for attack,
It's always when we're weakest.
We're down and then he's on our back,
When our outlook is the bleakest.

He'll get us through temptation,[158]
Our family he'll divide,
Our church destroy with gossip,[159]
Or scuttle us with pride.[160]
He'll sow seeds of discontentment,
Or magnify a fault,
Whatever way he gets his prey,
Destruction will result.[161]

Don't just expect a beast with horns,
That lurks in dark of night.
Don't be surprised, he comes disguised,
As an angel arrayed in light.[162]
Never be complacent,[163]
Or underestimate his guile,
He'll flatter you with swelling words,[164]
From behind a deceitful smile.[165]

If preaching bold the gospel,
He'll snatch away the seed,[166]
You make a time to share the truth,
He'll feign an urgent need.[167]
As accuser of the brethren,[168]
And lies his native tongue,[169]
He'll discredit every word you say,[170]
To those you live among.[171]

And so that roaring lion,
At times makes life seem rough,
And though the damage may be real,
His roar is mostly bluff.
He knows that he's defeated,
He knows his time is short,[172]
He'll try to make us forget these things,
And that's when we get caught.

Relentless are his fiery darts,
Lift high that shield of faith.[173]
Your breastplate, Christ's own righteousness,[174]
Be girt about with truth.[175]
Take the helmet of salvation,
Your sword God's timeless Word,[176]
Your feet shod with preparation,[177]
Pray trusting in the Lord.

Remember oh dear soldier,
This verse worth more than gold,
Greater is He that is in you,
Than he that is in the world.[178]
Submit yourself unto the Lord,
Resist the Devil's spree,
Draw near to God, drink deep His Word,
And watch that dragon flee.[179]

Orthodoxy & Orthopraxy

Orthodoxy is right belief whereas orthopraxy is right practice. These should go hand in hand, that is, right belief should lead to right practice, but often there is a marked difference between what one believes and what one actually does.

But be ye doers of the word, and not hearers only, deceiving your own selves.

—James 1:22

Absolute Truth

The statement, "There are no absolutes,"
Nullifies itself.
For if there are no absolutes,
Then there's certain truth.
If every reading is misread,
Then this too is void.[180]
For language imposes structure,
And gives meaning to every word.

Mathematics clearly proves
That absolutes exist.
And laws of logic demonstrate
That truth can be possessed.
If words were arbitrary things,
Language would not persist.
When anyone denies this fact,
The truth is just suppressed.[181]

Suppression in whatever form,
Deludes the mortal mind.
Denying truth destroys all good,
And chaos is all you'll find.
Hiding truth however well,
Does not make it void.
It just blinds the darkened heart,
Which one day will be destroyed.[182]

So who defines the absolutes?
It can't be you or me;
For if I decide what things are true,
You may disagree.
And if you decide just what is true,
I can then deny.
Truth transcends the human realm,
Apart from you and I.

There's only one who claimed to be
The Truth personified;[183]
Who under public scrutiny,
Lived the perfect life.[184]
Witnesses confirmed His Word,
Many testified
That God came down and dwelt with man,
Fulfilling all prophesied.

Not all roads lead to Rome,
As some will wrongly teach.
There's only one way back to God,
That the Lord Himself did preach.[185]
He boldly claimed to be The Way,
And excluded any other.
Faith in Jesus Christ alone
Is the way back to the Father.

But some may say, how do you know?
There's religious leaders many.
Oh, yes, perhaps, but only one
With credibility any.
For none else died and rose again.
No none else raised the dead.
And none else foretold history
In detail until the end.[186]

Absolute Truth

Yes, Christ fulfilled prophecies
In birth, in life, in death,
And told us future happenings,
Which in time will come to pass.
Science has discovered disputed Bible towns.
When man thought the world was flat,
God told us it was round.[187]
Yes, only One in history who claimed to be the Truth,
Can certainly be trusted, leaving abundant proof.

God gives meaning to every fact,
History tells His plan,
Of the origin and destiny,
Of every single man.
God Himself unchanging, defines the absolute,
And every branch and discipline depends on God as root.
God defines both right and wrong,
There is no middle ground.
Ethics and morality, outside of God aren't found.

So next time someone tells you there are no absolutes,
Ask him how he knows he's right, ask him for the proof.
Show him even argument is futile at very best,
If on laws of logic argument does not firmly rest.
And laws of logic can't be proven yet are absolutely true.
Denying them won't change the facts or any point of view.
Show him that his world makes sense
Because God makes it so.
His heart can be enlightened and saving truth can know.

Only One Way

Humanity is innately a religious race.
With a thirst for perfection and to find our place.
Our many attempts were in earnest begun,
With destruction the result of all but one.
Communism promises a classless society,
In reality the masses are brought under tyranny.[188]
Socialism trains its citizens to laud
The government for solutions instead of God.[189]
Islam claims to be a religion of peace,
But only when the world is converted by force.[190]
Buddhism preaches that life is all suffering,
But its salvation is nihilism leading to nothing.[191]
Hindus have millions of gods they believe,
But karma determines a caste they can't leave.[192]
Atheism too is indeed a religion,
With self being god, deciding his dictum.[193]
The Bible asserts man's problem is within,[194]
That Jesus Christ paid the wages of sin.[195]
So many religions! I hear you say.
Not true, there's two, but only one way.[196]
Either man through his efforts will try to please God,
Whether Buddha, The State, self or Mohamed,
Or those who humbly repent and believe[197]
The gospel of Christ and salvation receive.[198]
You see all religions are summed up as thus:
Man attempting perfection or God saving us.

The True Gospel

Let me warn you of the gospel leaven.
It is offered to all as an express ticket to heaven.
It requires no repentance or change in one's life.
A mere confession will simply suffice.
Thousands are sold, auditoriums filled.
"Revival!" we're told, but where is the yield?
Many will come in that day and cry, "Lord!"
To be told to "depart" by the true Living Word.[199]

The true gospel, however, is good news indeed
To all who bear fruit from its precious seed.[200]
Its truth is transforming, its fruit will remain
As you die to your flesh and you're born again.[201]
'tis true indeed that it starts with confession—
A true recognition of one's sinful position—
Then repentance from all that God calls transgression
And faith in the Lord Jesus Christ for salvation.[202]

But once on the road of sanctification,
We must have a goal; we must know our mission.
We no longer belong to ourselves but to God.[203]
Our lives have been bought with His Son's precious blood.[204]
Our mission? To love Him—heart, mind, soul, and might![205]
And love is obedience and faith without sight.[206]
Unconformed to the world, renewing the mind,[207]
Conformed to His Son, by tribulation refined.[208]

If there is no desire to drink in His Word,
If there is no fire to see souls convert,
If the company of fools is better preferred[209]
Than being with others who love the Lord,
If the testimony of change does not thrill your soul,
If holy living is not your goal,
If you hate what God loves or love what God hates,
You're still lost in sin; there is no debate.

Be careful, my friend, of all that you hear.
Believing in God is only the start.
The demons believe and tremble with fear.[210]
The Holy Spirit must indwell your heart.[211]
Your will must submit to Jesus as Lord.[212]
Your way must be guided by His holy Word.[213]
Though you will fall, you will hate your sin.
Forgiveness is assured when you confess sin to Him.[214]

So examine yourself, if you be in the faith.[215]
Don't be deceived; make sure you have life.
Salvation is free yet has a high cost.[216]
We can't earn it through works, and it cannot be lost.[217]
But once we are saved, the difference must show.
The fruit of the Spirit over time should grow.[218]
A child of God must become like his Father[219]
And must be willing to live or die for his Savior.[220]

Response to the Gospel

People cannot truly comprehend salvation until they understand what they have been saved from. It is so shameful that we often do not even realize the extent of our sin until we see its consequences on others, usually our loved ones. But seeing our sin as a fleeting glimpse in the mirror of our loved one's tears is just the tip of the iceberg when compared to the offense of constant rebellion against the Holy God who created us for His pleasure and who suffers continually from our arrogant selfishness because we do not love Him with all of our heart, mind, soul, and strength, not to mention the way we continually break His other nine commandments.[221]

> Holy Lord, my heart will burst,
> I know not how to render praise,[222]
> Deserving wrath and being cursed,[223]
> Nothing worthy in me to save.
> A billion stars all take their place,
> All obey their ordained course.[224]
> Ocean waves shoreward race,
> Yet stop at the word of Thy mighty voice.[225]
> But me, I've sinned not once nor twice,
> But ever since my wretched birth.[226]
> I think I'm something when I'm dust,[227]
> So proud to think I've greater worth.
> Heaven would be glad the world
> Banished one as vile as me,
> To where the worm dies not nor the fire quenched,

To spend a lost eternity.[228]
But with one hand God held back wrath,
The other to me beckoning,
To gaze upon His holy Son,
And believe the day of reckoning.[229]
Rather sentenced to that place,
The Son of God bore all my wrath.[230]
Falling down upon my face,
Eternal praise is not enough.[231]
Emptied now of any shred,
Nothing good within to cling.[232]
I humbly bow my once proud head,
And worship my most gracious King.

FAITH

Faith is not insurance
To make things go our way.
It's obedient submission,
Every single day.
We take the good for granted,
As if it's ours by right,
And then are disenchanted,
When difficult our plight.[233]

We aren't free to manufacture
A god of our demands.
We have His revelation
Of His nature and commands.
Whether man is willing
To worship here and now,
Every tongue shall confess
And every knee will bow.[234]

God owes us humans nothing.[235]
Our very breath's a gift.[236]
Because we pray to Him,
We expect an answer swift.
If He shows us mercy,
Our praise to Him we give,
But if he sends us trials,
It's His prerogative.[237]

More than Meets the Eye

We often throw a tantrum
Or silently we sulk
Like a faithful father,
Manipulation doesn't work.
Though we may entreat Him,
And humbly make appeal,
We must accept whatever comes
As His sovereign will.

God is not vindictive,[238]
He knows what we need best.
We're told to "cast our cares on him,"[239]
And trusting in Him rest.[240]
Live by faith and not by sight,[241]
And to this promise cling,
To His children all works for good.[242]
So give thanks in everything![243]

The Street Preacher

(This poem is dedicated to Guy Howell, the late Hubert Kimber, and all faithful Rundle Mall street preachers in the heart of Adelaide, South Australia.)

He stands on the corner as the city rushes by.
His heart bursts with passion; the people hear his cry.
His message ever urgent, ever nearer till they die:
"'Every man is guilty,' says the God who cannot lie!"

Thirty years ago, he would have drawn a crowd.
People once would listen, but they think he's crazy now.
Since the time he started preaching, morals have declined.
Now people want religion but not the Christian kind.

Some still take a tract from his ever-outstretched hand,
His preaching heard above the din of a Hare Krishna band.
He pauses momentarily to separate a brawl
As people pass oblivious to the violence in the mall.

"A tract, sir?" he queries to another in the crowd.
A hand grabs the gospel tract and casts it to the ground.
Unperturbed, he goes on preaching, his message ever strong.
His love for his Redeemer is what carries him along.

Once a City of Churches, now the Festive State,[244]
We forgot the source of freedom, the foundation that made us great!

More than Meets the Eye

We're high on a bough, perched proudly, chainsawing faster and faster.
As the branch we sit on weakens, we're unaware of the pending disaster.

Along comes a warden from the local council band,
"It's time to move on preacher, or in the clink you'll land."[245]
A far cry from bygone days, when policemen thanked the men
For keeping crime rate at a low through the gospel's message then.

Still the message goes forth weekly, ever faithful, ever clear,
To a city growing weary, which lives in constant fear.
He prays that perseverance will conquer in the end,
That the gospel's power will transform hearts and overcome the sin.

Though fruit seems few and far between, one saved in all those years,
He prays and preaches faithfully, with many, many tears.
Yes, God shall show more mercy to Sodom than this place,
As the glorious gospel message has been treated with disgrace.

But he stands on the corner as the city rushes by.
His heart bursts with passion; the people hear his cry.
His message ever urgent, ever nearer till they die:
"The day of grace shall one day cease, then judgment from on high!"

Always Somewhere Else

Praying for the missions in a distant jungle land,
Wishing to be of service—oh, to be there would be grand!
While our culture crumbles round us, like a castle made of sand,
Our focus is always somewhere else; our salt here is so bland!

A worker home on furlough speaks the circuit round.
With indifferent armchair interest, we listen to his sound.
Our churches here are shrinking, our testimony marred,
Our vision always somewhere else but in our own back yard.

Our youth are with us in body, their hearts already gone;[246]
The elderly are retired, disconnected from the young.
The middle aged are child-free, enjoying prosperity.
Our children are molded by the state instead of by the family.

The church is disintegrating and ravished by the wolves,
The family likewise fractured by socialism's goals.
Community is corrupted, through deifying self.
Our gaze is fixed across the seas at a mission somewhere else.

We've lost a generation to humanism's lies.
The roaring lion snatched them, right before our eyes.[247]
We didn't see it coming, unaware of his device,[248]
Distracted by a brighter star, a mission somewhere else.

I'm not opposed to missions; we're to preach to every land.
But we must not neglect the work here; the lost are all around.
The schools now teach religion, the humanistic brand.
Though once in a Christian nation, the church has lost her ground.

When we think of tithing, we have a one-track mind;
We think the only worthy cause is the missionary kind.
But gospel truth is far more broad than a ticket to the sky.
It's teaching the relevance of God's Word to all of life applied.

Little do we realize that there'll be no one to pay the bill
Of missionaries overseas if we continue down this hill.
Mission work begins at home, indeed within our house.
Support the Christian work right here, not always somewhere else.

EROSION

Before you or I can remember,
In the northern hemisphere winter
When the heathen celebrated the solstice
And the birth of the so-called sun god;[249]
The syncretistic Christians were party
To this abominable and pagan idolatry,
And thus was introduced Christmas
To forge Christian and pagan harmony.

With the hippie movement rock music was born.
And Christians avoided this rebellious thorn.
Not many years later we heard rock in the church.
Now it is accepted as if always the norm.
Cinema and other entertainment as well,
Used to be seen as coming from hell.
Christians avoided the ways of the world,
And holidays were used to worship their Lord.[250]

God gave roles to man and woman
That for thousands of years were the family's foundation.
The man provided, protected, and led,
The woman bore children and took care of the home.[251]
When a nation invaded, the Bible taught,
That women stayed home while men went and fought.[252]
Today we send women to the battle lines
And say it's just keeping up with the times.

Long hair was given to the woman for glory[253]
And yet on a man God declares it a shame.[254]
Modest dress was commanded from the start of history,[255]
Now immodesty in the church brings down God's name.
We are taught from the pulpit that we really shouldn't care
About our manner of dress or the length of one's hair.
We are taught it doesn't matter about a thing's origin,
As long as to fellow man we show true religion.

As the Jews made groves and high places,
They forsook God's pattern of worship.
Consenting to the nation's embraces,
They began to enjoy pagan fellowship.
Gradually, gradually as time passed by,
What was once held as truth they began to deny.
Then slowly, so slowly, a lie was believed,
Until by few the truth was received.

This is the pattern of history through,
And is the reason we must study how custom became.
For without knowing why we believe what we do,
Truth's boundary may be shifted and we'll be to blame.[256]
God's standard hasn't changed from the beginning of time,
Yet each generation admits a new crime.
We fail to pass on His Word to our children[257]
And thus they are ignorant of a practise's origin.

Yes, it matters how it started, the things we accept.
To pass on God's Word we must not neglect.[258]
What now seems so harmless may have begun
As direct disobedience to God's only Son.
Time doesn't diminish what He called abomination,
Even if it's practised by an entire nation.
The boundary must not move to suit our day,
For this is how truth is eroded away.[259]

Creation vs. Evolution

More than just atoms banging around,
Order and beauty and patterns abound.
Emotions and feelings, the human mind,
Can't be explained without being designed.

The simplest of atoms is a mystery to man.
And a cell is not simple, but a factory grand.
DNA isn't random; it holds vital instruction,
Which defines a species and its reproduction.

A cat will never give birth to a dog.
A prince will not emerge from a frog.
Each kind is unique. It can't interbreed.
Evolution is wrong. When will you concede?

Millions or billions of years, it's the same.
No length can accomplish evolution's claim.
Even eternity is not enough time
To generate man from primordial slime.

You can't have a heart beating alone,
Or a piece of liver evolve on its own.
Evolution of life has no defence,
It's all or it's nothing, or it doesn't make sense.

More than Meets the Eye

Geology shows no transitional forms.
The "missing links" were found to be false.
Examining the evidence there is but one choice.
All things cry "design" with a unified voice.[260]

Birds migrate to a distant land.
Animals know when danger is at hand.
Bees build hives with incredible skill.
Life is much more than material.

No big bang, but a spoken command
Brought forth the sky, the sea, and the land.
God created all in six literal days.[261]
Men deny to avoid giving Him praise.

Man was created in the image of God,[262]
He is no descendent of any primate.
His status is higher than anything made,[263]
But his rebellion plunged him into a ruinous state.[264]

Seashells scattered on mountain peaks
And fossils of sea creatures far from the beach.
Evidence of water and torrents of mud
All telltale signs of a global flood.

Yet the truth of creation and the flood are suppressed
By man's deeds of depravity and unrighteousness.[265]
Through history God has preserved His Word.
The Bible indeed is a two-edged sword.[266]

The Bible told us that the earth was round,[267]
Long before Columbus set sail.
History reveals through providence profound.
It continues to confirm, God's Word will prevail.

Creation vs. Evolution

He tells us our origin, how we were made.
He tells us we wilfully disobeyed.
He promised a Saviour, His birth prophesied,
So that when He came, He'd be recognized.

Lord Jesus Christ fulfilled every prediction—
From the place of His birth to His crucifixion.
His manner of life, the words He would say,
Even His resurrection on the third day.[268]

Perceive His design with every sense.
Examine closely the evidence.
The Bible tells history from beginning to end[269]
And holds the key to salvation, my friend.[270]

Environmentalism

"Save the trees!" "Save the whales!"
"Save the bears!" The cry prevails!
"Save the reefs," the shout rings shrill
As pollution spews from Ady Gil.[271]
Animals jealously guard their own,
But man's protection is misdirected.
When seal and unborn child are compared,
Guess which one is not protected?

"Your carbon footprint!" the vehement cries
As another aborted baby dies.
Is man the cause of climate change?
Or are these socialism's evil lies?
On large families they cast the blame,
As humans cause this devastation.
From having children we must refrain,
Until there's zero growth of population.

Vegans too who think it cruel,
To kill and eat an animal,
Next time you eat a plant for lunch,
You just might stress it as you munch.[272]
If you become a cannibal,
You'll save both plant and animal,
And reduce that "pesky" humankind,
Giving you your peace of mind.

Environmentalism

If we're results of chance and time
And man is equal to the worm,
Don't brush your teeth, we came from slime;
You were once a helpless germ.
Why really fret, oh, human beings?
After all, we're not to blame.
Survival of the fittest means
The weak die out and the strong remain.

"Social justice" is their plea.
But justice comes from Christianity.
Evolution gives us no such term.
It can't explain our deep concern.
Justice, love, and deep affection
Don't evolve from blind selection.
Human dignity and meaning
Come from a transcendent being.

It's God who made us like Himself
And bestowed on us the highest worth[273]
To work the land and enjoy its wealth,[274]
To take dominion of the earth.[275]
God does not reside in trees
Or dwell in temples made of stone.
You can't by earthly works appease;
Above the heavens is His throne.[276]

Consider pantheism's plight:[277]
Cattle roam about the street,
The starving don't survive the night
Because they dare not eat the sacred meat.
The river floods their mud-hut homes,
While at their temple made of stone,
To their river god they prostrate bow,
Afraid to dam its mighty flow.[278]

More than Meets the Eye

Christians must take earnest heed
To eliminate this noxious weed
When saving earth is a higher goal
Than one man's hell-bound, dying soul.
Careful stewardship, for sure!
But don't lose sight of why we're here.
Conserve indeed the mineral store,
But worship God and preach with fear.

Be a Man of Your Word

Be a man of your word!
Mean what you say.
Think twice before speaking,
Before committing your way.
Be a man of your word!
It's too common today
To go back on a promise,
To forget what we say.

When Isaac blessed Jacob,
Though Jacob deceived him,
His blessing was binding;
It could not be retracted.
Though Esau repented,
The blessing was given.
Though Esau wept bitterly
It was bound in heaven.[279]

Then Jephthah the warrior
Vowed that he'd offer
The first one to meet him
If God helped him win,
His dear only daughter
Came dancing with timbrels.
He still kept his promise,
Though it crushed him within.[280]

More than Meets the Eye

Words flow like water;
It happens too often.
We promise our help,
We promise to pray.
We'd do well to remember
Each idle word uttered;
We must give an account
At the great judgment day.[281]

Christianity by Name

All smiles,
No trials,
No empathy,
No sympathy,
You pour out your heart,
They'll pray for you.

Prayer is the modern excuse for inaction.
No practical help, just a verbal reaction.
From meeting to meeting,
From sermon to sermon,
Hearing God's Word,
Forever learning.

Prayer is powerful,
Don't get me wrong.
And God answers prayer
Of the faithful one.
But God gives his children responsibility
And He'll do the things which are beyond our ability.

We study God's Word to put into action
The faith and the love, to show true religion.
It's not just to listen and analyse
While others need help and agonize—

The orphan, the widow,
Deaf, blind, or lame,[282]
The struggling, the weak
With a flickering flame.[283]

There are those who are persecuted
For doing God's will.[284]
There are those who are isolated
Or continually ill.
There are others who through no fault of their own
Suffer depression, forever alone.

Then there are those who are ever so strong
Who never have hardship or feel alone.
To them the road is ever so smooth.
Promising help is the extent of their love.
When it comes to the crunch, it's too often the same,
They are only words, Christianity by name.

Have you ever noticed who lends the hand?
The ones who have suffered, who understand.
The ones who themselves are struggling along.
They recognize need requires more than a song.
They give what they can from what little they have,
And though it's not much, it's given in love.

Even the Lord washed His disciples' feet[285]
And talked to others whom no one would greet.[286]
He touched the leper, held the small child,[287]
Had compassion on those whom had been left defiled.
He gave up His life, answered the call.
He lived what He preached, a servant of all.

Christianity by Name

I urge you, oh, brethren, by the mercies of God,
Consider the ways of our Master and Lord,
A visit, some time, a practical hand.
Christianity would awaken in this desert land.
It's more than just meetings, or we meet in vain.
It's action, or it's only Christianity by name.[288]

Textbook Christians

I wrote this poem after observing how Christians (including myself) are so quick to have an answer to people's problems and how our sympathy can be so superficial. When we lost our daughter Esther, I realized just how much I did not previously understand about grief over the loss of a child. I recalled our hollow words of sympathy to a neighbour who lost a child years before. What I want to communicate in this poem is that you will have more success in your endeavours to reach people if, rather than having a terse one-line answer for all of their problems, you have a wealth of experience to draw upon from your own life's trials and express this in an honest and real manner. "Jesus" is not a Band-Aid for superficial wounds. He is the regenerator of the spirit and Lord over all. He is Lord of our emotions, which means that we must make these subject to Him. But even this does not mean we do not express our feelings. It just means that we should not sin in doing so. Whilst our spirit may be regenerated in Christ, it still dwells in this earthly tabernacle, which Paul describes as perishing daily.

—2 Cor. 4:16

I've been a Textbook Christian.
I can point you to a verse.
I don't have love or compassion,
But I have an answer terse.

Knowledge is not wisdom.
We need both to have effect,
Doctrine and experience,
Through trials that afflict.

Textbook Christians

We're not experts on everything,
Just because we know a verse.
We need to check the context,
In the Scriptures ourselves immerse.

The Lord Jesus had compassion.
He loves in deed and word.
To have one without the other,
Makes our faith absurd.

Let's not be textbook Christians,
But those who in God's hand,
Endure trial and persecution,
That we learn to understand.

Then with love and sensitivity,
Come alongside hurting ones
And show them from experience,
That we're qualified to comfort them.

If we're unable to empathise
With someone deep in grief,
It is better to say nothing,
Than use cliche for relief.

Orthopraxy

Love isn't love until it is tested.[289]
Faith isn't faith until it is rested.[290]
Trust isn't trust until it's invested.[291]
Humility is pride until self is divested.[292]

Be kind not only to those who are nice.[293]
Sacrifice is worthless unless it comes at a price.[294]
Treat others as you would have them treat you.[295]
If you judge others, prepare to be judged too.[296]

Temptation isn't sin, if it is resisted.[297]
Forgiveness can't apply until you've repented.
Patience is impatience until you have waited.
Words without action are always negated.[298]

Christian Cliques

Have you ever visited a well-established church gathering and found it impossible to break into the circle and have folks genuinely desire to get to know you?

Can I break into your circle?
Will you let me in?
I'm looking for some friendship,
To be known for who I am.

This circle is unbroken,
Has been so for many years.
A newcomer pays a visit
And discreetly disappears.

There's lots of talk of love
And fellowship so sweet,
But I feel like I'm a stranger,
Alone out in the street.

I may not have charisma.
I'm quiet and even shy.
That doesn't mean I'm aloof,
That you should pass me by.

I may not wear a smile.
I'm worn out by life's demands.
I'm yearning for real unity,
A family that understands.

More than Meets the Eye

It's hard to express my feelings
To open up and share my mind.
You penalize me for being me.
Why are you so unkind?

You don't want to get to know me
Because I tell it like it is:
The treacherous world around us,
The times in which we live.

The Lord was a man of sorrows,[299]
No laughter or making sport.
He recognized the pain of life,
And the numerous hearts that hurt.

Superficial chatter
Is as far as it ever goes,
And the things that really matter,
No one really knows.

Oh, family of the living God,
The hypocrisy makes Him cringe.
Don't talk of love and fellowship
And ignore those on the fringe.

CRITICAL?

You say that I am critical,
And indeed this may be.
But what I say to you,
I also say to me.

If we know the truth
It is sin if it's not done.[300]
Ignorance may be bliss,
But knowledge excuses none.

It's easy to close an eye
And pretend that we don't see
The worldliness that abounds
In the Christian community.

But while many won't speak out,
And instead would rather hide,
The Word of God is a two-edged sword,
Joints and marrow it will divide.[301]

One says we're not to judge
And it's just your point of view.
God's Word commands we prove all things,[302]
And evil to eschew.[303]

More than Meets the Eye

So if I cry against something
Know I'm guilty too.
And God's standard applies to me
As it applies to you.

So when we see that things aren't right . . .
That God's Word is disobeyed,
Whoever it is that's in the wrong,
Let the truth not go unsaid.

I expect that if you see
Me compromise the way,
That you too will speak out.
For my conviction, you will pray.

Know of a truth that it is so
When one law we break,
That we are guilty of them all.[304]
We fall short, make no mistake.[305]

You may break this law
And I may break another,
But in God's eyes all have sinned
And need forgiveness from the Father.

My weakness you may not have,
And yours may be my strength.
But a weakness is a weakness.
Shun pride at any length.

CRITICAL?

This does not mean though
That correction is taboo,
But speaking truth in love
Is what we have to do.[306]

What should we expect then
From someone who bears God's name?
Surely he should depart from sin[307]
And from appearance of evil abstain.[308]

I Am Nothing (without Love)

Though my sermons be eloquent,
Without love I'm just noise.[309]
Though my doctrine be "faultless,"
Without love it's all void.[310]
Though my faith can move mountains,[311]
I give the poor all I have wrought,[312]
Though as a martyr I'm burned,
Without love I am naught.[313]

When I'm unkind or impatient,[314]
Or easily annoyed,[315]
If envious or proud,[316]
My testimony is a fraud.[317]
If I'm arrogant or rude,[318]
When I think I'm "something!"
If I push my agenda,[319]
I'm unloving and thus nothing.

Some think love is just sentimental affection.
They say it's unloving to give any correction.[320]
Others avoid it, preaching fiery doctrine,
With heartless detachment and without any compassion.[321]
But both extremes undermine God's Word.
They render the power of the gospel absurd.
God's nature was manifest in His incarnate Son,[322]
It is love pure and true to those who respond.[323]

I Am Nothing (without Love)

A response to God's love must be true repentance.[324]
To wipe out the debt, to commute the death sentence.[325]
But once in His family, to be like our Saviour,
Must be the desire of every believer.[326]
Love is a decision which results in an action,
To not render evil when that's our attraction.[327]
For every believer, true love is vital:[328]
By love shall the world know who is His disciple![329]

Christian Liberty

The question is not how close can we get
Before we fall off the edge,
But how will this choice impact my heart?
Do I need to be near this ledge?
Scripture may be silent and yet,
It's not that simple, you see,
The outcome of a particular choice,
May not be good for me.

Each decision has a consequence,
With only a few results:
It will either draw me nearer to God,
Or increase my number of faults.
Even if it may not appear
That an action will cause offense,
If it doesn't enhance my Christian life,
Then pursuing it doesn't make sense.

Too often today we hear those words,
"It's Christian liberty."
But freedom in Christ is freedom from sin,
To serve Him unreservedly.[330]
So if a choice we make doesn't further this goal,
Though lawful, it may not be expedient.[331]
We must be careful, redeeming the time[332]
With testimony pure and evident.[333]

Christian Liberty

Too often we edge so close to the fire,
Excusing our dangerous affection.
The truth being that selfish desire
Is our genuine motivation.
We may be able to deceive ourselves,
But others are not quite so blind.
God knows the heart with its deceptive power,[334]
And may chasten until we're refined.[335]

So let us ask the right question today,
Lord, what is good for my progress?
How can I make full use of my time,
To glorify you with my substance?
How can I encourage and build up another?
May I take care not to stumble
A weaker child of God in the faith.
Lord, how I need to be humble.

My Master and Lord, let me comprehend,
The truth of my liberty.
That I am no longer a slave unto sin,
But to serve you, I am now free.
Let all that I do be to that end,
Let it endure thy refining fire.[336]
May thy Word guide every choice,
That thy will be my deepest desire.

Gluttony

One fruit of the Spirit is self-control.³³⁷
And we've heard many sermons about alcohol.³³⁸
But rarely, if ever, do we hear or see
A preacher speak out against gluttony.³³⁹

A sensitive issue, we're afraid to offend.
It's far too common and it's a rising trend.
Lamentable, avoidable, a shameful tragedy,
Our culture is dying of morbid obesity.³⁴⁰

We're not overpopulated as many falsely say,
When half our food is wasted every single day.³⁴¹
Just take a look around you when you're at the food court,
Half full plates discarded without a second thought.

Food in mass production, abundance on the shelf,
Frenzied vast consumption, gratifying self.
Greed is now so common, unrecognized its blight,
Gluttony leads to poverty³⁴² and more illness now our plight.³⁴³

We seek quick solutions for our numerous afflictions,
And are rarely reproved to quit our addictions.³⁴⁴
Our no-fault culture goes to great lengths
To divorce an action from its consequence.³⁴⁵

So rather than addressing a problem's root cause,
We treat the symptoms with a bandage and gauze.
But God is not mocked; we'll reap what we sow[346]
Of the destructive results of no self-control.[347]

In the church we're no different, a blind spot in our view,[348]
We concentrate on other sins while gluttons fill the pew.
Obesity leads to lethargy and laziness to nonchalance,
The call goes out for laborers, with little to no response.

Affluence was once our friend to help us in the work.
Complacency is now the end of many in the church.
Self-denial must be taught, starting very early.[349]
The goal of work and gaining wealth is for God's kingdom,
not our belly.[350]

Culture Transformers

Are we culture transformers?
God wants nothing less.
Do we help raise the standard,
Of language, demeanour, and dress?[351]

Taking every thought captive
To the obedience of our Saviour and Lord,[352]
Even our very attitudes
Must come from Him, not the world.[353]

What statement is made by our presence?
Are we one who merely survives?
Can observers quickly determine
Who is Lord of our lives?

Do we love truth and proclaim it[354]
Or perpetuate Satan's lies?
Are we beacons of light in the darkness[355]
Or contributing to the church's demise?

The heart above all is deceitful,[356]
The truth we're quick to pervert.
God rewards the fruit of our doings,
Not our intention or fleeting thought.[357]

Culture Transformers

He tries the reins with His testing,[358]
To see just where our loyalty's found.
Are we ready and willing to obey Him?
Too often excuses abound.

How often our verbal profession,
Promises that roll off our tongue,
Declaring our total surrender,
Yet blending with those we're among.[359]

We dare not look or sound different,
We might stand out in the "grey."[360]
We may even feel some rejection,
We'll just be a Christian on Sunday.

But this is what it really comes down to,
Whom will we make Lord of our life?[361]
We either follow the Saviour,
Or the liar and father of strife.[362]

Preaching the gospel in word and in action,
Living proof of God's infinite wisdom,
Prepared for the onslaught of man's opposition,[363]
Ready with answers for his inquisition.[364]

Ambassadors crying for repentance within,[365]
Being careful we don't fall into the same sin.[366]
Watching and praying, with a motive of love,[367]
Wise as a serpent, harmless as a dove.[368]

Willing to show pure religion,[369]
Providing for the need of the widow and orphan,[370]
Judging the fatherless, relieving the poor,[371]
Saving the oppressed from their callous torture.[372]

More than Meets the Eye

Eyes are continually on us,
Even if we don't know it and yet,
We're always discipling others,
So often it seems we forget.³⁷³

Let's not leave anyone guessing,
There's no room for a life compromised.
There really is no such position,
As a Christian living disguised.

If you love God you'll love His commandments,
And make every effort to obey.³⁷⁴
For observers there should be no confusion.
The difference should be like night versus day.

Are we culture transformers?
Of this goal we must never lose sight.
The Bible not the world as our standard,³⁷⁵
To see the transformation of salt and of light.³⁷⁶

MODESTY

When sin first entered the human race,
God called Adam and he hid his face.[377]
So God dressed them both in coats of skin.[378]
To hide their shame, to cover their sin.[379]

Adam thought aprons of fig leaves would do.[380]
But God set the standard for me and you.
We must search His Word for guidance for dress.
Not copy our culture nor second guess.[381]

Today there's no shame, just look around.
Exposure's a game, widespread and profound.
Our consciences seared, we don't think it's wrong.[382]
We need to take stock of those we're among.[383]

Moses declared God's will for a distinction,
God called cross-dressing an "abomination."[384]
Women should not wear what pertains to a man,
And vice versa is true, this is God's command.

The Apostle Paul wrote more of the same.[385]
Swapping the hair lengths was obvious shame:
Short hair on a woman, long hair on a man,
The confusion of gender derides God's plan.

More than Meets the Eye

Modesty is more than just how to dress,
It's sobriety and shamefacedness:[386]
No fluttering eyelids, flattering lips,[387]
Pretentious comportment, clamorous quips.[388]

God's roles for each gender were also defined,
With social destruction if they're undermined.[389]
This is not about whether the sexes are equal.[390]
But a division of labour designed to be helpful.[391]

As Christians it's time to renew our mind,[392]
Not follow the culture, just running blind.
Our Master has spoken. We have His Word.
Being indifferent is mocking our Lord!

Life's Extremes

For, lo, the winter is past,
The rain is over and gone;
The flowers appear on the earth;
The time of the singing of birds is come.[393]
Weeping endures for a night,
But joy comes with the morning light.[394]
There's a time to weep and a time to laugh.[395]
These are the extremes along life's path.

In the day of prosperity be joyful.
But in the day of adversity consider:
God hath compared the one to the other,
That we should remember our Creator.[396]
How quickly forgotten is God's kind provision,
His answers to prayer and His constant protection.
Regardless then of our daily condition,
Circumstance shouldn't dictate our dedication.

Why is it that prayer is most fervent
When diverse trials are evident?
Why must God command our attention,
Through His provident intervention?
"I love you" are words that are easy to say,
When nothing challenges or opposes our will.
Praise comes easy when things go our way,
But when God is silent, praise decreases to nil.

More than Meets the Eye

If only our prayer was consistent.
If only our pleading as vehement
As it is when it's tough and we fall on our knees
And cry out to God with the most earnest pleas.
If only praise flowed as freely in trials
As it does when life is laughter and smiles.
If only we loved Him with all of our being
And worshipped Him with zeal independent of feeling.

God is worthy of our deep adoration.
His glory abounds in all of creation.
Regardless even of His gift of salvation,
We owe Him our life from its very foundation.
In spite of extremes we experience each day,
We must show Him due honour whenever we pray.
The problem is we don't comprehend His great name,
And minimize our Lord in a manner profane.

But now, ignorance is past,
Excuses are valid no more.
His glory fills all the earth.
The time for renewal of the heart has come.
Confession is due every night,
But joy comes with the morning light.
Faithfulness whether we weep or laugh,
In spite of extremes along life's path.

Taste and See

Enjoy Him with every sense.[397]
Worship Him with reverence.[398]
Thank Him for life's pleasures.[399]
Set your heart on heavenly treasures.[400]
Trust Him to meet all your needs.[401]
Follow wherever He leads.[402]
Obey Him implicitly.[403]
Wait for Him patiently.[404]
Confess sin in humility.[405]
Overcome triumphantly.[406]
Praise Him with psalms and hymns.[407]
Build carefully with precious gems.[408]
Serve Him diligently.[409]
Love Him unreservedly.[410]
Testify faithfully.[411]
Contend for the faith earnestly.[412]
Speak of His wondrous works.[413]
Be consumed with His awesome thoughts.[414]
Meditate on His written Word.[415]
Taste and see that the Lord is good.[416]

Perseverance

Every worthy cause
Takes effort and hard work.
When you feel like giving in,
It's then you mustn't shirk.
Whether it takes a day,
A week, a month, a year,
Take one step at a time.
You must persevere.

Have you ever sat and watched
Another win a prize
And felt the disappointment . . .
Tears welling in your eyes?
If only you'd continued
And hadn't given in,
You'd have the satisfaction
Of persevering to the end.

Before you commit yourself
To any plan of action,
Seek the will of God,
To know it's His direction.
If it's not His plan for you,
Don't even waste your time.
Persevering down that path,
Is effort that's in vain.[417]

PERSEVERANCE

If you know that it's God's will,
It's sin if left not done.[418]
Even if no one else obeys,
And you're the only one.
Keep your eyes upon the Lord,
Press on and have no fear.[419]
You must always do what's right.
Through the hardship persevere.

Remember the salmon that swim upstream
Against the opposing torrent,
Tirelessly toiling to reach their goal,
Their determination is clearly apparent.
Not eating for days as they journey home,
Oblivious to injurious debris.
No opposition will deter their travail,
A lesson for you and me.

We're living in a disposable age
Of instant gratification.
We aren't used to waiting,
Or showing moderation.
This breeds impatience,
From the earliest of years,
As a generation learns to give in
And never perseveres.

God is never mocked.
We'll reap just what we sow.[420]
Whatever seed we plant,
That's exactly what will grow.

More than Meets the Eye

If we really want the fruit,
It takes more than words sincere.
We'll reap if we faint not,
If we truly persevere.[421]

When others just give up
Or won't even try,
When others see the cost
And think it's just too high,
Keep pressing forward.
Don't be troubled by your peers.
Reward will only come
To the one who perseveres.

Fulfilment

The eye is not satisfied with seeing,
The ear never filled with hearing.[422]
No possessions can fill the lust of the flesh,
No riches or ecstatic feeling.
The preacher instructs the reader well,
Who investigated wisdom and folly,
The search for fulfilment without the Lord,
Is vexation of spirit and vanity.[423]

To eat and to drink and to make his soul,
Enjoy the good in his labour,
This gift is from the hand of the Lord,
For a man there is nothing better.[424]
Godliness with contentment we're told is great gain.[425]
The simplest of all life's pleasures:
Enjoy your children, the wife of your youth,[426]
For these are priceless treasures.

There's no need to journey to find yourself,
Such travel will be in vain.
Take heed to his warning, the words of the wise,
There's no need to experience the same.
The preacher made the conclusion clear,
You'll be happy if you understand this:
For this is the whole duty of man,
To fear God and keep His commandments.[427]

Every Good and Perfect Gift

What wondrous, glorious, priceless gift, have we not destroyed?
The splendour of creation, we've trashed and rendered void.
Face-to-face relationships we've traded for a screen,
A garden walk, its smells and sounds, replaced by movie scene.[428]
God's wholesome and organic food we drain of nourishment,
We wilt the spinach, age our meat, and call it excellent.[429]
Majestic beauty we discard, promoting the grotesque,[430]
Noble virtues mocked and scorned, while lewdness is expressed.[431]
Civility is old fashioned, extolling the profane,
We celebrate the vulgar and think holiness insane.[432]
Melody and harmony we've exchanged for noise and chaos,[433]
Immorality not purity is now our culture's ethos.
The Ten Commandments given us, as bounds for our protection,[434]
Are shackles we fight vehemently, to society's destruction.
Love we have perverted, confusing it with lust,[435]
Covenants we have broken, violating trust.
Marriage is discarded for frequent temporal flings,
We reject God's gift of children, instead preferring "things."[436]
We drown out rationality with drugs and alcohol,
And disregard pure logic to the damnation of our soul.
Wisdom tried and tested we discard as out of date,
Preferring fads and fashions which too often seal our fate.
Words exact and eloquent we've stripped of any meaning,
So truth is now decided by an arbitrary feeling.
Good is now called wicked and wicked means good instead,[437]
Whatever God has given us we've turned upon its head.
Every good and perfect gift we've thrown back in His face,[438]

And yet in spite of all we've done He offers us His grace.[439]
Behold our heinous treachery against the King of Heaven,[440]
Ungrateful, wretched, loathsome beasts, how far indeed we've fallen.[441]
Lord Jesus came in love to pay the penalty for sin,[442]
Our response to God's most precious gift? We mocked and
    murdered Him.[443]

Ever Mindful

The thorns with which God cursed the ground
Because of Adam's sin,⁴⁴⁴
Were twisted into Lord Jesus' crown,
And cruelly thrust on Him.⁴⁴⁵
Iron nails He'd used for years,
Driven through His hands.⁴⁴⁶
The wood He worked with, cut, and shaped,
His crucifixion stand.⁴⁴⁷

His occupation tangibly
A reminder of His plight,⁴⁴⁸
Lovingly revealed to man
When breaking bread that night.⁴⁴⁹
Ever mindful of His death
To save the world from sin,⁴⁵⁰
He set his face as a flint
Toward Jerusalem.⁴⁵¹

Never flinching though He knew
The pain He would endure,⁴⁵²
For one repentant sinner,
Salvation to procure.⁴⁵³
Falling down upon His face,
Sweat like drops of blood,⁴⁵⁴
The agony of all my sin
Borne by the Son of God.⁴⁵⁵

Ever Mindful

It was no surprise that painful night,
Betrayed by Judas' kiss,[456]
He knew full well what lay ahead,
He came to earth for this.[457]
Though all creation should have known,
To worship when He came,[458]
He was not welcomed by His own,[459]
But spat upon and slain.[460]

For which good work did He deserve
A criminal to die?[461]
He'd healed the sick and raised the dead,
Restored the blinded eye.[462]
The wrath of God deserved by us[463]
Should be understood,
When we consider just what we did,
To the holy Son of God.

But well before He graced this earth
With His countenance,[464]
We'd mocked and scorned His matchless worth
In disobedience.[465]
The day that Eve exchanged God's truth
For the devil's lie,[466]
We deserved the wrath of God
And began to die.[467]

Though incomprehensible,
He left His Father's throne[468]
To dwell amongst ungrateful man,
To make cursed earth His home.[469]
Though we're undeserving of His grace,[470]
He freely shed His blood.
Such is the love and mercy
Of the righteous Son of God.

Thank You, Lord

Thank You, Lord, for loving me,
Before I knew You existed.[471]
Thank You, Lord, for saving me,
The chief of sinners attested.
You give purpose and meaning to everything made,
Your wisdom is marvellously and richly displayed,
Not a speck in all space can another claim stake.
Not a second of eternity Your knowledge escape.
How foolish and proud to even consider,
That without You we possibly could ever be better.

Thank You, Lord, for Your precious Word,
It is better than infinite treasure.[472]
Thank You, Lord, for Your presence sure,
That no distance nor peril can sever.[473]
My heart cries out with a yearning so strong,
To consecrate my life to Lord Jesus alone.
No matter the road or the mountain steep,
To live by faith and Your commandments keep.
For living life without regard to Your will,
Is utter futility and totally nil.

Thank You, Lord, for my dear wife,
For the privilege and honour of marriage.
Thank You, Lord, for my children,
Each one a blessing so cherished.
My prayer is that all my progeny will

Thank You, Lord

Worship, obey, and live faithfully, till
With a shout and the voice of the archangel strong,
The Lord Jesus comes to call us all home.[474]
But till the day of that most glorious sound,
May I be a man of integrity found.

Thank You, Lord, for my blindness,
Yes, even this disability.
Thank You, Lord, for each trial.
You've told me that they are good for me.[475]
For if I had sight, the lust of the eyes,
Perhaps I'd be damned, Your Word I'd despise.
I know of a truth that all You allow
Is for Your purpose, though we may not know how.
I accept my lot as Your choicest of ways,
And render to You the most reverent of praise.

Epilogue to the 2009 Edition

At the age of thirty-seven years and six months, I finally learned what a rainbow actually looks like. My six-year-old son made a plasticine model of a rainbow and for the first time in my life I discovered that the colours are actually layered one upon another as arcs of colour, rather than dividing a single arc into segments. I was so surprised when my wife described to me the appearance of the rainbow as I felt my son's model. It was also humbling to receive this profound truth from my little child. It is significant that God allowed me to learn this truth after having written this book and selected the picture for the front cover. It would be absolutely absurd for me to continue to believe in my false concept of reality now that I have been confronted with the truth.

May we all have the humility and honesty to accept truth when the light of Scripture exposes our ignorance or false assumptions, rather than remaining in darkness. May we also accept the light of God's precious Word upon each of our paths with gladness and gratitude as it exposes areas of our lives which need to come under the Lordship of Christ. Then, may we respond to that light in willing and immediate obedience to the glory of our Lord and Saviour, Jesus Christ, the master poet.

—Joseph Stephen

Epilogue to the 2015 Edition

The godless have observed that the pen is mightier than the sword.[476] Indeed it is the pen which preserves knowledge for future generations provided it is read and comprehended. Prior to the Reformation and the printing press, when the Word of God was obscured, being unavailable in the common tongue, men were controlled by the withholding, filtering or reinterpreting of truth. They were kept in ignorance at the whim of the priests and academics.

During the bloody years of the translation of God's Word into English, many died defending the right of all to read the truth in their own tongue. Christians risked all and endured incredible hardship in order to obtain just one copy of God's priceless revelation to mankind because they discovered that the truth certainly set them free.[477] The novelty of the printed word in English did not last long however. We soon lapsed into spiritual darkness again as Satan tried a new tactic, inundation and indoctrination.

Over the past four hundred years or so we have been utterly deluged with printed material. Indeed the truth revealed by Solomon was made manifest: "And further, by these, my son, be admonished: of making many books there is no end; and much study is a weariness of the flesh."[478] Much of this material however has not exalted but suppressed the truth.[479] While knowledge has increased[480], wisdom has been lost in the cacophony of voices, though "she crieth in the chief places of concourse[481]."

Modern "visionaries" (after this world's definition) such as Karl Marx, John Dewey, Jean-Jacques Rousseau, and even

Adolf Hitler knew of the power of the written word, a tool far more powerful than any sword-driven revolution. Indeed, as social engineers they indoctrinated the masses in order to control them and create a socialist society in which every child would ultimately become an automatic evangelist for their definition of truth. This indoctrination has been so successful that the majority of the church of this generation has grown up in their clutches and has accepted their socialist views by default. They then use this lens to read and interpret the Word of God, rather than letting the Word of God shape their interpretation of culture. Since study is a weariness of the flesh, it is much easier to blindly accept the so-called undisputed truth revealed by academics than to discern truth through our own evaluation of facts. In fact, we have been schooled as to what to believe and think rather than being educated in how to think and thus discern what to believe.

The tide has come full circle. Most Christian households now have multiple copies and multiple translations of the Holy Bible. In spite of this, we now observe a generation of Biblical ignorance of the grandest scale, not because we do not have the written revealed truth, but on the contrary, we have been drowned in literature, so much that we close our eyes and read nothing at all, or, blindly accept the first thing we read as gospel. Academics, under the power of the prince of darkness, have again relegated the masses to ignorance by deconstructing language and indoctrinating an entire generation through what they call public schooling and the media.

My plea is that we, as parents, would raise a generation that has been taught discernment; not what to think, but how to think as we once did. We must raise a generation of readers who are able to discern what is worth reading and what is worth burning, to discern the agenda of the writer from the truth rather than accepting the package wholesale. The only way we can possibly navigate the labyrinth of modern rhetoric

Epilogue to the 2015 Edition

is to again wholeheartedly believe that the Holy Bible, as originally translated, is the ultimate and undisputed God-breathed revelation of truth by which all of reality must be judged, and to believe that every born-again believer who is filled with the Holy Spirit can be empowered with discernment, and be led into all truth if they humbly and genuinely submit their own will to the all-knowing, all wise, impeccably holy, Almighty God of all truth.[482] How we need to repent for our utter apathy, complacency and practical disdain toward God's most precious, life transforming, civilization sustaining, Word of truth.

    I have updated this volume to continue journaling my thoughts concerning the issues of our day in the form of poetry, analysing such issues from a Biblical perspective. I pray that my contemplation may impact your life, and the lives within your influence, by directing your focus back to the two-edged sword which proceedeth from the mouth of the living Word.[483]

Endnotes

1. Eph. 2:10 – Workmanship is translated from the Greek word *poiema,* from which we get our word poem.
   Strongs, 4161, *poiema:*
   a. that which has been made
   b. a work
   c. of the works of God as creator
2. Luke 12:34; 2 Tim. 4:8.
3. Gen. 2:21-24, 3:16; Ex. 6:14, 6:25, 18:25; Num. 1:16, 7:2, 13:3; Deut. 1:15; Josh. 14:1, 19:51; 1 Cor. 11:3, 11:9; Col. 3:18-19; Eph. 5:22-25; 1 Peter 3:1.
4. Gen. 3:17-19, 30:30; 1 Tim. 5:8; 2 Thess. 3:10.
5. Gen. 14:12-16 (Abraham rescues Lot); Num. 32:6, 32:16-27 (children of Gad and Reuben fight but leave their children and wives in the protection of fenced cities); 1 Sam. 30:5-18 (David rescues Abigail); Prov. 22:3-5; Neh. 4:14; Mark 3:27; Luke 11:21 (describes the strong man protecting his house); God Himself is referred to as a strong tower (Ps. 144:2), shelter (Ps. 61:3), refuge (Ps. 9:9, 14:6, 46:1), protecting wings (Ps. 17:8, 36:7, 57:1), rock, fortress, deliverer (Ps. 18:2), hiding place, and shield (Gen. 15:1, Ps. 3:3, 28:7, 32:7, 91:4, 115:11, 119:114).
6. Gen. 17:19; Prov. 1:8, 13:1, 15:5; Eph. 6:4.
7. Mal. 2:15.
8. Ps. 128:3.
9. Ps. 128:3, 127:4.
10. Ps. 144:12.
11. Eph. 5:28-29; Eccl. 9:9.

12. Titus 2:5; 1 Tim. 5:14.
13. "The Hand That Rocks The Cradle Is The Hand That Rules The World" by William Ross Wallace 1865.
14. Ps. 113:9; Prov. 31:10-31.
15. Eccl. 12:13; Josh. 22:5.
16. Eph. 6:4.

    The definition of *nurture* from Thayer's Greek Lexicon (emphasis added):

    paideia:

    a) The **whole training** and **education** of children (which relates to the cultivation of **mind** and **morals,** and employs for this purpose commands and admonitions, reproof and chastening). It also includes the training and care of the body.

    b) Whatever in adults cultivates the soul, especially by correcting mistakes and curbing passions.

    c) Instruction that aims at increasing virtue.

    d) Chastisement, chastening (of the evils with which God visits men for their amendment).

17. 2 Tim. 2:24.
18. 1 Tim. 4:12.
19. Prov. 23:26.
20. James 1:5.
21. Prov. 14:15.
22. Prov. 14:12, 3:5-6.
23. Prov. 29:18.
24. Welcome Noah Issachar Stephen, our eighth blessing from the Lord, born naturally at home on 24 July 2010 after three prior caesareans.
25. "The Hand That Rocks The Cradle Is The Hand That Rules The World" by William Ross Wallace, 1865.
26. Mark 3:25.
27. Gen. 2:24.
28. Matt. 19:6.

29. Eph. 5:22.
30. Eph. 5:25.
31. Prov. 4:23.
32. 1 Cor. 12:26.
33. Eph. 5:23-29.
34. 1 Peter 3:7.
35. Col. 3:19.
36. Gen. 2:18.
37. 1 Cor. 11:3; 1 Peter 3:6; Neh. 4:14; Num. 32:16-27.
38. Prov. 14:1.
39. Prov. 31:10-12, 26.
40. Prov. 31:30.
41. Prov. 21:19.
42. Prov. 26:21.
43. Prov. 27:15.
44. James 1:20.
45. Heb. 13:4.
46. Mal. 2:15.
47. 1 Peter 3:4; Prov. 31:10-31.
48. 1 Cor. 16:13.
49. Proverbs 4:1-27, 23:26.
50. "Education is thus a most powerful ally of humanism, and every American public school is a school of humanism. What can a theistic Sunday school's meeting for an hour once a week and teaching only a fraction of the children do to stem the tide of the five-day program of humanistic teaching?" (Charles F. Potter, "Humanism: A New Religion," 1930).

    "The battle for humankind's future must be waged and won in the public school classroom by teachers who correctly perceive their role as the proselytizers of a new faith: A religion of humanity – utilizing a classroom instead of a pulpit to carry humanist values into wherever they teach. The classroom must and will become an arena of conflict between the old and the new – the rotting corpse of Christianity, together with its adjacent evils and misery, and the new faith of humanism." (John J. Dunphy, "The Humanist" (1983).

"There is no God, and there is no soul. Hence, there are no needs for the props of traditional religion. With dogma and creed excluded then immutable truth is also dead and buried. There is no room for fixed, natural law or permanent moral absolutes."

(A Common Faith, John Dewey, page 51, Yale University Press, 1934.)

"You can't make Socialists out of individualists—children who know how to think for themselves spoil the harmony of the collective society which is coming, where everyone is interdependent." (John Dewey)

"Submit yourself to the State, and my philosophy will liberate you from submission to intermediate authorities like the Church and the family." (Jean-Jacques Rousseau)

"I am much afraid that schools will prove to be great gates of hell, unless they diligently labour in explaining the Holy Scriptures, engraving them in the hearts of youth. I advise no one to place his child where the Scriptures do not reign paramount. Every institution in which men are not increasingly occupied with the Word of God must become corrupt." (Martin Luther)

51. *The Children of Caesar: The State of American Education* DVD by Dr. Voddie Baucham, Jr. (http://www.gracefamilybaptist.net/store/product/children-caesar/).

IndoctriNation: Public Schools and the Decline of Christianity in America DVD by Colin Gunn (http://www.colingunn.com/).

Already Gone, copyright © 2009 by Ken Ham, Master Books (www.answersingenesis.com).

52. Proverbs 22:6; Ephesians 6:4. Note definition of nurture (παιδεία) is the total training of mind and morals for all of life.
53. 1 Timothy 5:8; Titus 2:5.
54. Genesis 2:18.

Endnotes

55. Malachi 4:6.
56. Ps. 139:13-16.
57. Gen. 1:26-27.
58. Isa. 44:2, 44:24, 49:5; Jer 1:5; Ps. 139:13, 22:9-10, 71:6; Eccl. 11:5; Job 10:10-11; Gal. 1:15.
59. http://www.prolifeaction.org/faq/unborn.htm.
60. Ps. 127:3-5.
61. John 1:14.
62. Mark 10:16.
63. Mark 10:14.
64. Being totally blind, as I was growing up, I was often made to feel like a burden on society, to the point where I felt like ending my life. During those dark times, if someone had offered euthanasia, I may very well have taken up the offer. Now, however, God has richly blessed me and I am learning to live with my disability even when made to feel burdensome. I have learned that my worth is determined by God and not my achievements or usefulness as a human.
65. Ex. 20:13.
66. Gen. 1:27.
67. Ps. 127:3-5, 128:1-4; Gen. 17:6, 17:20, 24:60, 28:3, 41:52, 49:25; Deut. 7:13.
68. Jer. 32:35; Lev. 18:21. R. J. Rushdoony, *The Philosophy of the Christian Curriculum*, pp. 112-113, describes the essence of the worship of Moloch as Statism.
69. Matt. 19:14; Mark 10:14; Luke 18:16.
70. Prov. 10:4, 12:24, 13:4, 22:29; 2 Thess. 3:10.
71. Ps. 37:25.
72. Luke 23:29.
73. Gen. 1:28, 9:1, 9:7, 35:11.
74. A search on www.google.com for "overpopulation myth" will result in numerous articles exposing this satanic lie.
75. Ex. 1:9-20.

76. http://www.thewitness.org/agw/pusurinkham.121901.html; http://gvnet.com/childprostitution/USA.htm.
77. Globally there are more slaves today than at any time in human history. An estimated 27 million men, women, and children are living in bondage. In 2007, slave traders made more profit than Google, Nike, and Starbucks combined. http://www.mannafreedom.com/get-informed-about-human-trafficking/what-is-human-trafficking/
78. http://www.destinyrescue.org/aus/countries/thailand http://www.toonaripost.com/2012/08/us-news/startling-ohio-sex-trafficking-report-released-this-week/
79. Jeremiah 17:9; Psalm 10.
80. The Leadership Survey on Pastors and Internet Pornography suggests that 37 percent of pastors have an issue with this sin. Other sites suggest much higher figures (above 50 percent). See http://www.christianitytoday.com/le/2001/winter/12.89.html. When this is compared to the number of pastors who actually read their Bibles regularly, is it any wonder? The following site suggests that only 38 percent regularly read their Bible for personal devotion and personal study: http://www.intothyword.org/articles_view.asp?articleid=36562. We truly need another reformation and you need to be part of it!
81. Prov. 13:20.
82. Mal. 2:15.
83. Prov. 5:3-23, 6:23-35, 7:6-27.
84. The richest, strongest and godliest men of Scripture all fell, so, don't take the warning lightly. See 1 Ki. 11:1-4; Judg. 14:1-20; 2 Sam. 11:1-24.
85. Mal 2:14-16; Mat. 19:5-9.
86. Prov. 31:10-31 cp 1 Ki 16:31, 18:4, 19:1-2, 21:7-25; 2 Ki. 9:7-37; Rev. 2:20.
87. Mal. 2:15; Ps. 128:3-4, 113:9; 1 Tim. 5:14; Tit. 2:5.

Endnotes

88. Mat. 6:33.
89. 1 Tim. 6:11.
90. 1 Pet. 3:7.
91. 1 Pet. 3:3-4; 1 Tim. 2:9.
92. Mat. 6:21.
93. Prov. 29:25; Mat. 10:28.
94. Gen. 24, 28:1-2, 34:9; Deut. 24:1; Ezra 9:12; Neh. 10:30; Prov. 24:27; Jer. 29:6; 1 Cor. 7:27.
95. 2 Tim. 2:15; 1 Thes. 4:11; Tit. 2:6-8.
96. Eccl. 4:12.
97. Prov. 23:26.
98. Ps. 78:2-8; Ex. 13:14; Ps. 44:1; Deut. 6:20.
99. John 14:2-3.
100. Eph. 2:8-10.
101. Heb. 12:2-3.
102. 2 Cor. 4:17.
103. Prov. 22:6.
104. Gal. 6:7.
105. Luke 11:7.
106. Isa. 28:9-10.
107. Exodus 20:15.
108. I know. My sister Rachele Suzanne Rowlinson was murdered on 29 March 2013 at Eudunda, South Australia.
109. Exodus 20:13.
110. Exodus 20:16.
111. At the time of the writing of this poem, Julia Gillard was Australia's first woman Prime Minister. Though she once professed Christianity, she is now an atheist. She was the first Prime Minister to be living in open sin (Isaiah 3:12).
112. *Truth and Transformation* by Vishal Mangalwadi ©2009 YWAM Publishing.

113. Preamble to Australian Constitution, 9 th July 1900: "humbly relying on the blessing of Almighty God . . . ."
114. Rom. 13:1-7.
115. Ps. 12:8, Pr. 13:34.
116. Preamble to the Australian Constitution.
117. The Greens are the fastest growing political party in Australia. They are a Socialist movement hiding behind the guise of Environmentalism. Their policies are anti-Christian and outright abominable. On their propaganda is a picture of the Dalai Lama.
118. Matt. 10:33.
119. Rom. 14:12, Matt. 12:36.
120. 1 Tim. 2:1-2.
121. Ps. 78:4-8.
122. In my neighbourhood, as I was growing up, my street was filled with families whose children played together and whose parents had cups of coffee together and visited each other. In my neighbourhood where my children are now being brought up most children are in childcare and parents rarely see each other, let alone visit each other for coffee. The decay in the family unit is also much more apparent as demonstrated by the description of my immediate neighbours in the stanza to which this note is attached.
123. *Lord of the Flies* by William Golding, Edmund L. Epstein, Mass Market Paperback, Berkley Publishing Group, July 1959, demonstrates what happens when children are left alone to govern themselves.
124. This page compares real minimum wages in the 1920s to those in the late 1990s and concludes that real wages have dropped by more than half. "Young couples complain that it now takes two wages to live in the suburb where their parents survived comfortably on one wage . . . . The business world, then, has acquired two workers for one family wage, where it used to get only one worker for that amount." *The Essence of Feminism* by Kirsten Birkett, p. 23, Matthias Media, 2000.

Endnotes

125. Titus 2:3-5.
126. By splitting the atom it is possible to use a few kilograms of uranium to create the explosive and destructive power of many thousands of kilograms of dynamite. So too, when a family, the atom of society, is split, the destruction of that and subsequent generations is devastating.
127. Isa. 53:3.
128. Matt. 26:55-56; Matt. 27:46.
129. Heb. 4:15.
130. WAXMAN, Daryl Paul. Passed away suddenly at home on September 6, 2014. Aged 56 years. Dearly loved son of Ramon (deceased)and Joyce Waxman. Loving brother of Alison and Geoff, Priscilla, Valerie and Barry, uncle to Sam and Leasa, Charlotte, Jacob, great-uncle to Ava. A life spent caring for others. Now at Peace (http://tributes.adelaidenow.com.au/notice/73132065).
131. When children are very young, unless the park has fences around it, one needs to be so careful that they don't run toward a road, go near the edge of an unsafe piece of equipment, walk in front of a swing, etc. With older children this is not as difficult, but it is impossible to do this safely alone, especially if there are other strange children at the park. A blind person cannot always orchestrate his environment to be exactly how he needs it to be in order to function.
132. While a totally blind person can cook, taking over the cooking in the middle of the task is not so easy since in order for the blind person to know how near something is to being cooked he usually relies on timing. Sighted people don't generally care about timing, but just see that something is cooked. Also, it's not so bad if when living by yourself you occasionally have half raw meat, but you don't want to serve this to little children.
133. A nappy is the Australian term for diaper.
134. Rachele Suzanne Rowlinson 1969-2013. (http://www.heavenaddress.com/Rachele-Suzanne-Rowlinson/437092/)
135. Esther Ruth Stephen 19-21.7.2004 (See Five Jewels).

136. My blindness was not diagnosed until I was about two years old. I then had about 2.5percent vision in one eye and none in the other. Because of my vegetative state in these first couple of years, I was diagnosed with Cerebral Palsy. Doctors told my mother I would never stand up or be able to feed myself. In fact I had great difficulty keeping down food until I was much older. By God's miraculous grace, here I am at forty-two, having defied their predictions. Over time and with intense physiotherapy and incredible dedication, my mother was able to help me gain motor skills, the ability to sit, stand, walk, feed myself, and eventually become a senior software engineer. I don't think there is any sign left of the brain damage that was evident during those first few years. My blindness, however, became worse over time until by the age of eighteen I was totally blind.
137. Isaiah 46:9-10; John 3:16; Psalm 139:2-4.
138. 2 Corinthians 1:3-5, 4:8-18, 12:7-10.
139. Proverbs 24:16.
140. James 4:1-3.
141. Ezekiel 33:11; Jeremiah 9:24.
142. Romans 8:28.
143. Luke 19:37-40; Revelation 4:8-11.
144. Mark 15:19,20.
145. Luke 2:7.
146. Mark 14:50, 15:34; Psalm 22:11.
147. John 19:25-31.
148. James 2:10.
149. Genesis 1:31.
150. Mark 15:14; Luke 19:14; Mark 12:6-8.
151. Psalm 19:1-3; Romans 1:20.
152. Job 1:20-21; Ps. 49:17; 1 Tim. 6:7.
153. Ecclesiastes 9:2; Matthew 5:45.
154. R. V. Paul Richard Wheeler. Court File Number SCCRM 13-218, Exhibit P9.

155. Prov. 27:6, 14:15; Luke 22:48; 2 Sam. 15:1-6.
156. Eph. 6:12-18, especially 16-17.
157. 1 Peter 5:8.
158. Gen. 3:1; Mat. 4:1-11, 13:38-39; Luke 22:40; 1 Cor. 10:13.
159. Prov. 20:19; Mat. 7:15; Acts 20:29-31; Gal 5:15; James 4:1.
160. Prov. 11:2, 13:10, 16:18, 29:23; 1 Tim. 3:6.
161. Prov. 10:29; Php 3:18-19.
162. 2 Cor. 11:14-15.
163. Mat. 26:41; 1 Cor. 16:13.
164. Prov. 29:5.
165. Prov. 23:6-7, 27:6b.
166. Mat. 13:4, 13:19.
167. Luke 14:18-21.
168. Rev. 12:10.
169. John 8:44.
170. Gen. 3:1.
171. Gen. 19:14.
172. Rev. 12:12.
173. Eph. 6:16; 1 Pet. 4:12.
174. Rom. 3:20-23; 2 Cor. 5:21.
175. Eph. 6:14.
176. Eph. 6:17.
177. Eph. 6:15.
178. 1 John 4:4.
179. James 4:7-8.
180. Postmodernism is a philosophy which permeates most disciplines in the modern university. It is best described as a worldview declaring that there are no absolutes and no definite meaning to words. It declares that personal interpretation is what defines truth. "I'm glad that's true for you but it isn't true for me" is the catch cry. This is of course consistent

with the random chaotic theory of evolution preached by the Humanist religion.
181. Rom. 1:18.
182. Col. 2:8; Eph. 5:6; Rev. 20:15.
183. John 14:6.
184. 2 Cor. 5:21.
185. John 8:24, 8:58, 14:6; Acts 4:12.
186. Isa. 46:9-10.
187. Isa. 40:22; Eccl. 1:5.
188. Stephane Courtois, ed., The Black Book Of Communism: Crimes, Terror, Repression (Cambridge, MA: Harvard University Press, 1999); R.J. Rummel, Death By Government (New Brunswick, NJ: Transaction, 1994).
189. Dr. David Noebel, Understanding the Times : The Collision of Today's Competing Worldviews (Summit Press 2006), p. 338.
190. IBID pp325-328.
191. Vishal Mangalwadi, The Book That Made Your World: How The Bible Created the Soul of Western Civilization, Thomas Nelson, 2011, p99.
192. IBID. p363.
193. Charles F. Potter, Humanism: A New Religion, 1930; John J. Dunphy, The Humanist, 1983.
194. Rom. 3:23.
195. Rom. 6:23.
196. John 14:6.
197. Mark 1:15.
198. Rom. 10:9; John 3:16, 3:36.
199. Matt. 7:21-23.
200. Matt. 13:18-23.
201. John 3:17.
202. Rom. 3:23, 6:23, 10:9; Acts 2:38, 26:20, 4:12; 2 Tim. 2:19.
203. 1 Cor. 6:19-20.

204. 1 Peter 1:17-19.
205. Mark 12:30.
206. John 14:15, 1 John 5:3; 2 John 1:6; Rom. 1:17.
207. Rom. 12:1-2
208. Rom. 8:29, 5:3-5.
209. Ps. 14:1.
210. James 2:19.
211. Eph. 1:13.
212. Rom. 10:9.
213. Matt. 4:4.
214. 1 John 1:9; Prov. 24:16.
215. 2 Cor. 13:5.
216. Rom. 6:23; Luke 14:28-35.
217. Eph. 2:8-9; John 10:28-29.
218. Gal. 5:22-23.
219. Luke 6:40.
220. Matt. 10:37-39; Phil. 1:21; Acts 21:13.
221. James 2:10.
222. Romans 8:26-27; Revelation 19:4-6, 7:11-12.
223. Romans 3:10-19; Psalm 5:5, 7:11; John 3:18-20, 3:36.
224. Job 38:31-33.
225. Job 38:8-11; Mark 4:41; Amos 5:8.
226. Psalm 58:3, 51:5; Job 42:6, 15:16; Psalm 14:2-3.
227. Genesis 2:7, 3:19; Psalm 103:14.
228. Mark 9:47-48; Revelation 20:11-15.
229. John 19:5, 30; Matthew 27:46; Psalm 22:1; Romans 3:23-26; 1 John 4:10; Romans 5:8-12; 2 Corinthians 9:15.
230. 1 Peter 2:24; 2 Corinthians 5:21.
231. Revelation 7:11-12, 5:11-14, 4:8-11.
232. Isaiah 64:6.
233. Job 1:20-21, 2:10.

234. Php. 2:10-11; Rom. 14:11; Isa 45:23.
235. Dan. 4:34-35; Ps. 50:10-12; Isa 43:13.
236. Gen. 2:7; Job 12:9-10; Isa. 42:5; Acts 17:24-25.
237. Heb 12:9.
238. Eze. 33:11.
239. 1 Pet. 5:7.
240. Ps. 37:7.
241. Rom. 1:17; Gal. 3:11; Heb. 10:38; Hab. 2:4.
242. Rom. 8:28.
243. 1 Thes. 5:18; Ps. 50:14.
244. In its formative years, Adelaide, South Australia, was known as the City of Churches because there were more worshipers than could fit in the numerous chapels. Many of those chapels have since been converted to night clubs, hair salons and other icons of our materialistic and hedonistic culture. South Australia is now known as the Festive State because of its regular liberal and godless festivities.(See *Australia's Christian Heritage* by Dr Graham McLennan at http://nacl.com.au.)
245. The "Clink" is a colloquial term for jail.
246. *Already Gone* ©2009 by Ken Ham.
247. 1 Peter 5:8.
248. 2 Cor. 2:11.
249. Whilst I could have named the idol to make this stanza flow more naturally, I did not want to disobey the commandment given in Exodus 23:13, "And in all things that I have said unto you be circumspect: and make no mention of other gods, neither let it be heard out of thy mouth."
250. The word *holiday* originated from the two words *holy day*, a day on which God asked His people to remember His works, provision, salvation, etc.
251. 1 Cor. 11:3; Num. 30:3-8; Titus 2:5; 1 Tim. 5:14; Ps. 113:9.
252. Num. 32:26-27; Neh. 4:14.
253. 1 Cor. 11:15.

254. 1 Cor. 11:14.
255. Gen. 3:6-21, esp. v. 21, 9:22-27; Ex. 28:42; 1 Tim. 2:9.
256. Prov. 22:28.
257. Ex. 13:14; Deut. 4:9-10, 6:7, 11:19; Prov. 3:1, 6:20, 7:1, 19:27; Eph. 6:4.
258. 2 Tim. 2:2.
259. Jude 1:3; 2 Tim. 4:3; Titus 1:9.
260. www.creationresearch.net, www.icr.org, www.answersingenesis.org, www.drdino.com
261. Ex. 20:11; Gen. 1-3.
262. Gen. 1:27.
263. Ps. 8:6-8; Gen. 1:26-28.
264. Rom. 5:12.
265. Rom. 1:18-21.
266. Heb. 4:12.
267. Isa. 40:22.
268. Matt. 1:22, 2:5, 2:15, 2:17, 2:23, 3:3, 4:14, 8:17, 12:17, 13:35, 21:4, 26:56, 27:9, 27:35; John 12:38.
269. Isa. 46:9-10.
270. John 3:16, 3:36; 1 John 5:11-12; Rom. 3:23, 6:23, 10:9-13; Eph. 2:8-10; Heb. 9:27; Rev. 20:15.
271. A high-speed protest ship used to disrupt Japanese whaling.
272. Scientific research has shown plants can hear themselves being eaten: By Jonathan O'Callaghan, Published 22:30 AEST, 2 July 2014 (http://www.dailymail.co.uk/sciencetech/article-2677858/Bad-news-vegetarians-Plants-hear-eaten.html#ixzz36Mmt2LAl Accessed on 8 July 2014.)

    A report from the University of Missouri-Columbia stated that a collaboration of audio and chemical analysis found plants respond to the sounds caterpillars make when eating leaves. The study also concluded that plants respond to the sounds defensively.

"We found that feeding vibrations signal changes in the plant cells' metabolism, creating more defensive chemicals that can repel attacks from caterpillars," said Heidi Appel, senior research scientist in the Division of Plant Sciences at MU. The scientists tested the effect of other sounds, like gentle wind or nearby insects and compared these with the vibrations made by caterpillars munching on leaves. They found that the plants were able to distinguish feeding vibrations from other sounds, and reacted defensively by producing more mustard oils, a chemical that is unappealing to many caterpillars.

273. Gen. 1:27.
274. Gen. 1:28-30, 9:1-3; Deut. 8:18; Prov. 13:11; Eccl. 5:19.
275. Gen. 1:28.
276. Acts 17:24-31.
277. Pantheism is the belief that the universe (nature) and God are identical. Pantheists thus do not believe in a personal, anthropomorphic or creator god. The word derives from the Ancient Greek: *pan* meaning "all" and *theos* meaning "God." Although there are divergences within Pantheism, the central ideas found in almost all versions are the cosmos as an all-encompassing unity and the sacredness of nature. The Holy Bible, on the other hand, teaches us that the true God created the universe and thus is above it rather than part of it. We are to worship God, not His creation. (Gen. 1:1; Rom. 1:25).
278. *Truth and Transformation* by Vishal Mangalwadi ©2009 WYWAM Publishing.
279. Gen. 27:18-40; Heb. 12:16-17; Matt. 18:18.
280. Judg. 11:30-40.
281. Matt. 12:36.
282. James 1:27; Luke 14:12-14; Matt. 5:35-40.
283. Matt. 12:20.
284. Matt. 5:11-12.
285. John 13:3-17.
286. Luke 7:37-48; John 4:6-29, esp. v. 27.

287. Luke 5:12-13; Mark 10:13-16.
288. James 2:14-18.
289. The "I love yous," which so easily roll off the tongue are meaningless until this love is tested by the trials of marriage, which subsequently survives and blossoms. The very description of love given in 1 Corinthians 13:4-7 indicates that true love must withstand opposition to each of the attributes described in these verses. Love is patient, that is, puts up with something that would test one's patience. Love is kind, that is, when you are provoked. Love seeketh not its own, that is, denies its own rights in order that the other person is promoted above self, etc.
290. Our faith must be rested in the object in which we claim we believe, whether it be the chair we have faith will hold our weight or the God who demands our faith and indeed can't be pleased without it (Heb. 11:1-6). Faith is demonstrated by action (James 2:15-26). We demonstrate our faith in a chair by sitting on it, not standing before it expressing the virtues of its great strength and potential to hold our weight.
291. Until we invest trust in someone, trust is just a concept. We can't say that we trust someone unless we are willing to allow him to do something that will exercise that trust.
292. How easy it is to say that we are humble and yet this very statement demonstrates pride.
293. Luke 6:32-34.
294. 2 Sam. 24:24.
295. Luke 6:31.
296. Matt. 7:1-5.
297. Gen. 4:7; 1 Cor. 10:13; James 1:13-15.
298. James 1:22, 2:14-26.
299. Isa. 53:3.
300. James 4:17.
301. Heb. 4:12s.
302. 1 Thess. 5:21.
303. 1 Peter 3:11.

304. James 2:10-11.
305. Rom. 3:23.
306. Eph. 4:15.
307. 2 Tim. 2:19.
308. 1 Thess. 5:22.
309. 1 Corinthians 13:1.
310. 1 Corinthians 13:2.
311. Ibid.
312. 1 Corinthians 13:3.
313. Ibid.
314. 1 Corinthians 13:4.
315. 1 Corinthians 13:5.
316. 1 Corinthians 13:4.
317. Since love is all of these things and since action without love makes me nothing, my testimony is voided.
318. 1 Corinthians 13:5.
319. 1 Corinthians 13:4.
320. Matthew 7:1-5 is often cited as a reason not to judge but the context simply says that we must first ensure we're not guilty of something worse. It says that if we do judge, be prepared to be judged also. It is a caution, not a prohibition. This is brought out by verse 5 and confirmed by other scriptures, such as 1 Corinthians 5:11-13.
321. Guilty as charged, your honor. Mark 10:21, 8:2, 6:34, 1:41; Jude 1:22; 1 John 3:17; Hebrews 5:2; Luke 15:20.
322. 1 John 4:7-8, 4:16; John 1:14, 14:9.
323. Romans 2:4-11; Titus 3:4-8.
324. Matthew 3:8, 9:13; Luke 15:7, 24:47; Acts 11:18, 20:21, 26:20; 2 Corinthians 7:9-10; 2 Timothy 2:25, Hebrews 6:6; 2 Peter 3:9.
325. Romans 3:25; 1 John 2:2, 4:10.
326. Luke 6:40; Matthew 10:25.
327. 1 Thessalonians 5:15; Romans 12:21.

Endnotes

328. 1 John 4:8-21.
329. John 13:35.
330. Rom. 6:1-23, 12:11.
331. 1 Cor. 6:12, 10:23.
332. Eph. 5:16; Col. 4:5.
333. 1 Tim. 4:12.
334. Jer. 17:9.
335. Prov. 13:24; Heb. 12:6-7.
336. 1 Cor. 3:12-15.
337. Galatians 5:22.
338. Proverbs 20:1; Isaiah 5:11, 5:22; Ephesians 5:18.
339. Deuteronomy 21:20; Proverbs 23:21.
340. Global report: Obesity bigger health crisis than hunger by Danielle Dellorto, CNN December 14, 2012 summarizing report at http://www.thelancet.com/themed/global-burden-of-disease.

    Fourteen million Australians (70 percent) are overweight or obese. Obesity has overtaken smoking as the leading cause of premature death and illness in Australia. Obesity has become the single biggest threat to public health in Australia. Cardiovascular disease (CVD), diabetes, and chronic kidney disease (CKD) account for approximately a quarter of the burden of disease in Australia, and just under two-thirds of all deaths. These three diseases often occur together and share risk factors, such as physical inactivity, overweight, and obesity. (Noncommunicable diseases country profiles 2011. © World Health Organization 2011 www.who.int)

    Generation Fat: Kids as young as 10 getting heart disease By Marianne Betts, The Herald Sun, July 17, 2011 (http://www.perthnow.com.au/lifestyle/generation-fat-victorias-obesity-crisis/story-e6frg3pl-1226096504186)

    Maternal Mortality, why the rise? "... America's leading health professionals have attributed this rise to morbid obesity . . . diabetes," Caroline Brettingham, 25th June 2010.

Sydney Morning Herald, Obesity in pregnancy is dangerous: study. October 16, 2008.

Lisa M. Bodnar, Anna Maria Siega-Riz, and Mary E. Cogswell, High Prepregnancy BMI Increases the Risk of Postpartum Anaemia, Obesity Research (2004) 12, 941–948; doi: 10.1038/oby.2004.115.

"Australians have their heads in the sand about what obesity really means . . . this needs changing and fast before we see a generation with a lower life expectancy than their parents." The report warns that too many people across all ages are gorging on excessive portions and high-calorie convenience foods while failing to get enough exercise. A staggering 85 percent of a typical day is now inactive. (Plate of Our Nation report: http://www.plateofournation.com.au)

341. Let's end the global food waste scandal by Tristram Stuart, Special to CNN November 18, 2011.

(http://articles.cnn.com/20n11-11-18/world/world_europe_food-waste-london_1_food-waste-surplus-food-food-production?_s=PM:EUROPE)

Garbage bin analysis in NSW, Victoria, and South Australia shows that 40 to 41 percent of the contents of our household garbage bins is food. Overseas, the story is the same. Every single day, Britain throws away five million potatoes, a million slices of ham, four million apples, and seven million slices of bread.

(http://www.abc.net.au/environment/articles/2011/02/08/3123168.htm)

Food waste - Aussie households bin close to three million tonnes of food each year by Emily McCluskey28 Jun 2011 (www.choice.com.au)

342. Proverbs 23:21.

343. http://www.obesityinamerica.org/understandingObesity/diseases.cfm.

344. The scriptures speak of but one addiction favourably, see 1 Corinthians 16:15 kjv, the house of Stephanas who "addicted themselves to the ministry of the saints."

Endnotes

345. Take careful note how often blame is not placed where it belongs. When reporting about a car accident, reporters say, "The car ran off the road" rather than "The driver lost control."
346. Galatians 6:9.
347. Philippians 3:19; Titus 1:16.
348. Link between religion and being overweight, NSW academics find By Greg Stolz, The Courier-Mail, June 28, 2012: ". . . the "sin of gluttony" might not be frowned upon by religious people as much as other vices such as drinking . . . and that many religious celebrations might even encourage overeating."
349. Luke 9:23.
350. Genesis 1:26-28; Deuteronomy 8:18; Philippians 3:19; Romans 12:11; Hebrews 6:11-12.
351. 1 Timothy 4:12; Colossians 4:6; Titus 2:8.
352. 2 Corinthians 10:5.
353. Romans 12:2; Ephesians 4:22-24.
354. 2 Thessalonians 2:10; 3 John 1:4.
355. Matthew 5:14-16.
356. Jeremiah 17:9.
357. Jeremiah 17:10.
358. Ibid.
359. Isaiah 29:13.
360. 2 Corinthians 6:14-17.
361. Luke 16:13.
362. John 8:44.
363. Titus 1:9; 2 Timothy 2:25.
364. 1 Peter 3:15.
365. 2 Corinthians 5:20.
366. 2 Peter 3:17; 1 Corinthians 10:12; Galatians 6:1.
367. Matthew 26:41; 1 Thessalonians 5:17; Ephesians 6:18; Hebrews 4:15.
368. Matthew 10:16.

369. James 1:27.
370. 1 Timothy 5:3-16; Psalm 82:3; Jeremiah 5:28, 22:3; Isaiah 1:17, 10:1-2; James 1:27.
371. Jeremiah 5:28, 22:3; Isaiah 1:17, 10:1-2; Psalm 82:3; Galatians 2:10.
372. Isaiah 1:17, 58:6; Ecclesiastes 4:1.
373. 1 Timothy 3:7; 1 Thessalonians 4:12; Colossians 4:5; Philippians 2:15.
374. 1 John 1:6, 2:4, 2:15-16.
375. Psalm 1:1-2; 1 Corinthians 1:20, 2:6, 3:19.
376. Matthew 5:13-16.
377. Gen. 3:9.
378. Gen. 3:21.
379. Gen. 9:22-25; Lev 18:1-24, 20:10-21.
380. Gen. 3:7.
381. Nakedness was not just wearing no clothes but exposing what should be covered. For men and women this was different. If one compares Ex. 28:42 with Isa 47:2-3, men's breeches were to be at minimum from the loins to the thighs whereas women were considered naked if they exposed the lower leg. I.e. women were to cover to the ankle whereas it was acceptable for a man to gird up his loins, showing their lower leg (Job 40:7; Jer. 1:17.) Of course neither were to expose any of the upper half as demonstrated by God's coats of skin which covered from the neck to the ankle. (Also see 2 Sam. 6:14-20 where Michal describes King David as uncovered or naked though he wore a linen ephod.) Interestingly, Biblical history teaches that it was the man who could wear either a robe or breeches, but women only wore a robe. Today, women wear pants or a dress while men wear pants, a reversal of the past. At the height of the reformation, Christian women wore long dresses and Christian men wore pants. This is still universally recognized as the natural order amongst conservative Biblical Christians, and should remain the standard as it comports with Scriptural teaching on

the distinction, function and modesty of clothing acceptable to God. Also note the historical origin of blue denim jeans which may now be considered mainstream by the masses but which originated in the 60's rebellious youth culture. God's people should be careful to embrace what is considered mainstream without carefully considering origins and symbology. Nothing is neutral. What we wear, how we speak, who we mix with, tells the world a lot about our convictions and values. Christians should also take note that the Bible always speaks of appropriate apparel, i.e. a harlot was known by her attire as was a guest fit for a wedding (see Prov. 7:10 compare withMat. 22:11-13). Today, it is becoming more common in western culture to wear beach-ware to not only the beach, but the shops, and sadly, even church. When James speaks of not showing favouritism to a man in "vile raiment" in James 2:2-4, he is not condoning inappropriate attire for the children of God, only warning against partiality. There is a great difference between an unbeliever or poor person coming to a meeting in inappropriate raiment, and a mature believer who simply chooses to wear inappropriate clothing because it is the fashion of the prevailing culture. We must renew our minds indeed and study the Scriptures rather than the mainstream media.

382. 1 Tim. 4:2.
383. 2 Cor. 6:14-17; 2 Tim. 2:22.
384. Deut. 22:5. Many like to refer to the surrounding verses and argue that since these other things no longer hold for the church that neither should this isolated verse. The difference is that the surrounding issues are not called an abomination. An abomination to the Lord back then is still an abomination today. His standard doesn't change. (Ps. 119:89; Mal 3:6a; Heb 13:8).
385. 1 Cor. 11:14-15, 6:9; Also see Eze. 16:7; Isa 47:2. It was humiliation for men to grow their hair long as when fulfilling a Nazarite vow (Num. 6:5), or shave off their beards (2 Sam. 10:5).
386. 1 Tim. 2:9-15.

387. Prov. 6:25, 2:16, 7:5.
388. Prov. 7:11-12, 9:13-15; Eph. 5:4.
389. Judg. 4:9; Gen. 3:16-19; Tit. 2:5;1 Cor. 14:33-35; 1 Tim. 2:12-14; 1 Thess. 3:10; 1 Tim. 5:8; Prov. 31:10-21; Isa. 3:12; Rom. 1:26-28.
390. Gen. 1:26;Gal 3:28.
391. Gen. 2:18; 1 Pet. 3:7.
392. Rom. 12:1-2; Eph. 4:17-24, especially v23.
393. Song 2:11-12.
394. Ps. 30:5.
395. Eccl. 3:4.
396. Eccl. 7:14.
397. Eccl. 2:24, 3:13, 5:8; 1 Tim. 6:17.
398. Ps. 89:7; Heb. 12:28.
399. 1 Thess. 5:18.
400. Col. 3:2.
401. Ps. 18:30, 34:22, 37:5, 118:8; Phil. 4:19.
402. Ps. 23:2-3; Isa. 48:17; John 10:3.
403. 1 Sam. 15:22; Eccl. 12:13.
404. Ps. 27:13, 37:7.
405. 1 John 1:9; James 4:6.
406. Rom. 12:21.
407. Ps. 95:2; Col. 3:16.
408. 1 Cor. 3:10-13.
409. Ps. 119:4.
410. Josh. 22:5; Deut. 6:5; Mark 12:30.
411. 1 Peter 3:15.
412. Jude 1:3.
413. Ps. 145:21.
414. Isa. 55:8-9; Ps. 139:17, 94:19.
415. Gal. 6:9.

Endnotes

416. Eccl. 1:8.
417. Eccl. 2.
418. Eccl. 2:24.
419. 1 Tim. 6:6.
420. Ps. 127:3, 128:3-4, 112:1-3; 3 John 1:4; Prov. 5:18.
421. Eccl. 12:13.
422. Josh. 1:8; Ps. 1:2.
423. Ps. 34:8.
424. Ps. 127:1.
425. James 4:17.
426. Heb. 12:2-3.
427. Gal. 6:7.
428. Gen. 3:8.
429. Wilted spinach was offered as gourmet food at a local restaurant. Almost all butchers consider aged meat as superior though the Bible always speaks of eating meat fresh, as soon as it was slaughtered (Gen. 18:7-8, 27:14-17; Exod. 12:6-10; Luke 15:23.)
430. Socialist Goals 22 and 23 taken from *The Naked Communist*, by Cleon Skousen, 1958, read into the US congressional record 1963 by HON. A. S. HERLONG, JR.

    22. Continue discrediting American culture by degrading all forms of artistic expression. An American Communist cell was told to "eliminate all good sculpture from parks and buildings, substitute shapeless, awkward and meaningless forms."

    23. Control art critics and directors of art museums. "Our plan is to promote ugliness, repulsive, meaningless art."
431. IBID. Goals 26, 40 and 41:

    26. Present homosexuality, degeneracy and promiscuity as "normal, natural, healthy."

    40. Discredit the family as an institution. Encourage promiscuity and easy divorce.

    41. Emphasize the need to raise children away from the negative influence of parents. Attribute prejudices, mental

blocks and retarding of children to suppressive influence of parents.

Note just how many of these socialist goals have been achieved in our culture today.
432. Hosea 9:7-8.
433. See Hell's Bells 1st or 2nd ed. DVD by Eric Holmberg, from http://theapologeticsgroup.com/.
434. Exod. 20:1-17.
435. 1 Cor. 13:4-7.
436. Ps. 127:3-5, 128:1-4.
437. Isa. 5:20.
438. James 1:17. The gifts of nature, relationships, food, beauty, virtues, holiness, music, protective commandments, love, trust, marriage, children, reason, logic, language, wisdom, truth, and even His only begotten son, we have corrupted, desecrated, destroyed, scorned, mocked, perverted, rejected, in favour of a counterfeit or a figment of our own imagining.
439. Isa. 1:18.
440. John 1:11; 1 Cor 2:7-8; Isa 50:6, 53:3; Matt. 26:67; Luke 19:14.
441. Rom. 3:23; Isa. 55:9.
442. 1 John 4:9-10.
443. Matt. 27:35-50; Luke 18:31-33; Mark 15:20-39; John 19:17-37.
444. Genesis 3:17-18.
445. Matthew 27:29-30.
446. Mark 6:3; Matthew 27:35; Isaiah 49:16.
447. Ibid.
448. Ibid.
449. Luke 22:15-20.
450. 1 John 2:2; Hebrews 9:28; John 3:16-21, 3:36.
451. Isaiah 50:6-7; Luke 19:28-44.
452. Mark 8:31; Luke 9:22, 24:7.
453. John 13:7-8, 3:16-21.

Endnotes

454. Luke 22:41-44; Mark 14:32-42.
455. 1 Peter 2:24; Galatians 2:20.
456. Mark 14:43-45.
457. John 12:27.
458. Luke 2:25-38; John 4:25-26, 9:30-38.
459. John 1:11.
460. Mark 15:1-39.
461. John 10:32.
462. Luke 7:22.
463. John 3:36; Romans 1:18, 2:4-6.
464. John 1:14.
465. Psalm 2:1-3, 10:3-11.
466. John 8:44.
467. Genesis 2:17, 3:1-7.
468. John 5:36, 6:38, 6:57, 17:5; 1 Corinthians 15:47; Luke 3:22.
469. John 1:14.
470. Romans 3:10-23.
471. 1 John 4:19.
472. Ps. 119:72.
473. Heb. 13:5, Rom. 8:35-39.
474. 1 Thess. 4:16-18.
475. Rom. 5:3-5.
476. Edward G. Bulwer-Lytton, 1803-1873.
477. John 8:32-36.
478. Eccl. 12:12.
479. Rom. 1:18.
480. Dan. 12:4.
481. Prov. 1:20-23.
482. John 16:13, 17:17; 1 Tim. 1:17.
483. Rev. 1:16, 2:16, 19:15; Heb. 4:12; Eph. 6:17.

www.ingramcontent.com/pod-product-compliance
Lightning Source LLC
Chambersburg PA
CBHW031418290426
44110CB00011B/436